Dear Roy

With my best wishes!

Shana Tova.

[signature]

MY STORY

תולדות חיי

Rabbi Barry Marcus MBE

AMBERLEY

First published 2019

Amberley Publishing, The Hill, Stroud
Gloucestershire GL5 4EP

www.amberley-books.com

British Library Cataloguing in Publication Data.
A catalogue record for this book is available from the British Library.
ISBN 978 1 3981 0086 2 (print)
ISBN 978 1 3981 0155 5 (ebook)

Origination by Amberley Publishing.
Printed in Great Britain.

Acknowledgements

This modest book is for my family: my five daughters, my sons-in-law and my, to date, thirteen grandchildren, who are my source of pride and joy. It is you who, at various times, have urged me to put pen to paper.

– *Saba B.*

I would like to express my sincere thanks to my good and dear friend Steven Tucker for both encouraging me and assisting in bringing this book to print. In addition thanks to Nick Hayward and all at Amberley Publishing.

I also want to convey my deep gratitude to Raquel Amit who for many years was my trusted and efficient PA and who has helped immeasurably with this publication.

In memory of my dear beloved parents:
Rabbi Nochim Leib Marcus (5 Shvat 5746 – 14 January 1986)
Esther Marcus (2 Sivan 5777 – 27 May 2017)

Esther Marcus

Descended from a long, unbroken rabbinic dynasty dating back to Joel Sirkiss, Chief Rabbi of Krakow, and Rabbi David HaLevi Segal, Esther Marcus, who has died in Johannesburg, aged 95, had made the transition from Poland, to South Africa and London. She was the mother of Barry Marcus MBE, the dynamic rabbi of the Central Synagogue in Great Portland Street, London and was known for her warmth and quiet dignity. Her family had a long history in South Africa where Rabbi Marcus had served in one of Johannesburg's largest communities, and in Israel.

Esther was born in Slonim (then Poland, today Belarus) where her father Rabbi Shlomo David Grawitsky was a widely respected Torah scholar and a student of the Chofetz Chaim. Rabbi Grawitsky left Poland and made his way to Cape Town in 1929, followed a few years later by his wife Lieba, their two sons and daughter Esther. Rabbi Grawitsky was appointed Rabbi of Woodstock Synagogue and served on the Cape Town Beth Din. Esther was educated in Cape Town.

In 1939 Esther married Rabbi Nochim Leib Marcus, who had been a student of the famous Mir Yeshiva (a Lithuanian yeshiva in Mir, now in Belarus) and supported him in his role as Rabbi in Cape Town, for close to 50 years.

Her grandchildren describe her as quiet, humble and wise. 'Her Yiddishkeit was internalised and she had a deep love and dedication to Torah values. She was happy with simplicity and appreciated the important things, enjoying her grandchildren as much as she would enjoy an inspirational Dvar Torah. She was a true Eshet Chayil.'

Esther Marcus was known for her absolute commitment to her family and to traditional Jewish values. She conducted her life with quiet dignity and inner strength.

Tributes were paid to her true beauty which lay in the simplicity and integrity with which she lived her life. She is survived by four children Rabbi Barry Marcus, Shlomo, Ruth, Joseph, 13 grandchildren and 30 great grandchildren.

Jewish Chronicle, 11 August 2017

Esther Marcus: Born 21 November 1921. Died 27 May 2017.

Contents

בס"ד

INTRODUCTION

I was born on a Friday evening, Shabbat 28 October 1949, in the Booth Memorial Hospital, close to our small, humble family flat – No. 4 Maynard Mansions, Maynard Street, Vredehoek, Cape Town.

I was aware from an early age that our family was different to others in our area, and especially at school where very few children were observant – some may have had kosher homes, but very few were shomer Shabbat. My older brother Shlomo and I were probably the only ones with kipot, even though we attended a Jewish school – Herzlia.

Yiddish was the dominant language in our family, which consisted of my parents, my older brother Shlomo, my sister Ruth and my youngest brother Joseph ('Jase').

The background to my life really begins in Eastern Europe in Mir and Slonim in 1929. Two gentlemen who were to be my beloved zaides both left their families and met on a boat (a Union-Castle liner) and sailed to Cape Town in 1929. (For further details see page 14.) One was HaRav Shlomo David Grawitsky z"l from Slonim, whom I sadly only knew from his children and his immense reputation as a G-d-fearing Talmid Chacham, a student and disciple of the 'Chafetz Chaim'; the other, Avraham Aizel Marcus (Markiel/ Markielewicz) from Mir.

My earliest and most abiding memory of my childhood is our small, modest and spartan flat overflowing with Sefarim (Hebrew books) – many volumes over a century old, most from the 'Heim' (the old country – Eastern Europe) and many with a distinctive smell. My shared bedroom was in fact my dad's 'study'.

To this day my first instinct when visiting someone's home is to look for books. I'm aware of this almost involuntary reaction when I go into someone's home and do not see any books, or, more accurately, Sefarim!

Herzlia School was an adjustment. There were very few kipot, if any, other than Shlomo and I, and I still remember the discomfort at a young age being referred to as 'the Rabbi's son', etc.

Unlike most of my fellow pupils I walked to school, or very occasionally caught the bus, while others passed us – some in chauffeur-driven cars.

I looked forward to Bnei Akiva's weekly meetings, but especially the three-week summer camp, where I felt comfortable and not at variance with my peers. All at camp were at ease with our Jewishness. We had fun, but all davened and benched as a normal part of our lives.

Home was certainly different, but an incredibly enriching environment. I cannot recall seeing my late father without a Sefer (book) in his hand. He had an insatiable love of learning and a thirst for knowledge that was cultivated in his early years in his beloved and famed Mirrer Yeshiva, where he excelled as a student and built an enviable reputation as a Talmid Chacham (Torah scholar).

Yiddish was our home language, and Polish/Russian was only used when my parents did not want us to understand. In early childhood I developed a great affection for the richness of Yiddish and Jewish music, joining the shul choir at a very young age.

We regularly had fascinating guests, although as a young child I didn't initially appreciate that some of the greatest leaders of the last century were regular visitors in our small flat. On a number of occasions my bedroom was shared by the famed Ponevezh Rov HaRav Yosef Kahanneman, and the Rosh Yeshiva of Mir – Harav Chaim Finkel in 1963 and later HaRav Beinish Finkel. Waking up and seeing these revered 'g'dolei Torah' (Torah scholars), the hadrat panim, their radiance has left an indelible impression on me.

My dad was the dominant personality, so gracefully balanced by my dear mom, who was quiet, gentle and nurturing. They enjoyed a long, wonderful and respectful relationship.

I learnt an appreciation of nature from my dad, with trips to the zoo and secluded beaches in summer, and acquired a love of the outdoors. He introduced me to soccer, which piqued my interest in sport. I developed an interest and passion for it, especially rugby and tennis.

My school years were not especially inspiring, except for a few teachers. Playing sport in school was enjoyable and helped my social integration.

Mom was always nurturing and a most gentle and intelligent soul who also had a love of reading and an interest in politics, but was always softly spoken.

Osher (Grawitsky – Mom's younger brother and father of David, Renee and Seymour) lived with us for some time. He too was a wonderful and gentle soul, and introduced me to tennis and DIY.

Most Sunday afternoons were spent at the home of Bobbe and Zaide Marcus in Benjamin Road, Wynberg, where on average up to nine of their ten children would regularly gather – my dad, Leibel, being the oldest; Nechama, who lived in Warmbaths; Zalman; Chava (Eve – Stellenbosch); Shmuel (Sam); Moshe (Morris); Yudel (Joe); Leizer (Leslie); Masha; and Basha – along with wives, partners and grandchildren, often having over twenty in their modest home.

Bobbe Marcus was a real 'balaboosta' who always prepared a feast, not only on Sundays, but as there were always visitors there was 'heimische gerichten' (traditional treats).

Soon after my bar mitzvah I was 'farmed out' to different shuls, mainly to ones where they had no rabbi or chazan. I leined and davened on Shabbat and Yom Tov – fortunately my father had informally taught me, and being in the Vredehoek Shul Choir helped.

My first position was in Woodstock Shul, where my late grandfather, Rabbi Shlomo Dovid Grawitsky z"l, had served from 1929 until his death in 1944 and where his son Motel (Mordechai – father of Shlomo Dovid, Meishe, Chava and Dovie – Bnei Brak), my mom's brother, was the rov. I spent many a Rosh Hashanah and Yamim Noraim with Motel and Chava, sleeping at the Gelbarts'. I spent a year serving Rondebosch Shul on Shabbat where I stayed with Sam and Anne (parents of Rochelle, Brian and Charlene – San Diego). I also spent a year in Camps Bay Shul on Shabbatot, staying with Solly and Chana – Anne (parents of Larraine, Hazel and David – Canada).

Military service was compulsory and I was drafted into the army in early 1968. My late father arranged a transfer from Oudtshoorn, where there were no kosher facilities, to Youngsfield by writing to the then Minister of Defence, P. W. Botha (later prime minister of South Africa). We received a telegram from P. W. Botha confirming the transfer. The camp was a few miles from Bobbe and Zaide Marcus in Wynberg, and whenever I got leave I would walk and spend Shabbat with them. This was a special time that I remember very fondly.

I was faced with a dilemma after finishing high school – matriculation. I was awarded a scholarship to Bar Ilan University, where I spent four wonderful years in Israel (1968–72) and I also spent time in Ponevezh Yeshiva, where I was warmly welcomed by Rav Kahanaman. I spent most chagim in Jerusalem with the wonderful family of Reb Beinish Finkel.

While at Bar Ilan University, I could see the possibility of an academic future. I was elected to the Agudat Studentim (Student Union) and was sent to the USA as a representative of Israel's universities for a WUJS (World Union of Jewish Students) conference in 1970.

There was, however, pressure on me to return to South Africa. While in Israel I met the Chief Rabbi of South Africa, Bernard M. Casper, and I travelled after my graduation in August 1972 to Johannesburg, but turned down the position of university chaplain. Instead, I went to Cape Town to Herzlia School, where I was a Hebrew teacher from 1972 to 1974, and on the weekends and chagim I served the Arthurs Road Shul in Sea Point.

In 1975, I answered a call from Chief Rabbi Bernard Casper in Johannesburg to serve as his assistant and youth rabbi. I also began studying with Rabbis Kurtstag and Symanowitz at the 'Beit Midrash L'Rabanim' and lecturing in the Hebrew Department at Wits University.

I was married in October 1975 and soon thereafter, in early 1976, took up the position of minister at the Valley Observatory Hebrew Congregation and received semicha in 1979.

In July 1979, I accepted a call to be the rabbi of the Waverley Synagogue, one of the largest communities at the time in Johannesburg. Here I was also the principal of its Hebrew School, which had some 350 pupils at its peak.

As a result of a shocking tragedy – the death of the daughter of one of my congregants – I co-founded a crisis centre with Dr Allen Zimbler, which operated for many years, helping countless people with a variety of emotional and other issues. The centre was well received and gained a great deal of positive publicity in Johannesburg and nationwide.

In a very disturbing incident in September 1981 the fence of our house in Waverley was daubed with swastikas and spray painted with the words 'Joden Verboden' (Jews Forbidden). It was understandably shocking and caused much worry and anxiety, especially as by that stage we had three young daughters – Lieba, Aviviya and Ora (Gabriella and Eliana were born later).

In 1984, I began collaborating with my father after he suggested we write a book together, which would be called *Father and Son*. After my father's passing in January 1986, I completed the task and published it as a tribute to his memory.

Our family moved to Ramat Aviv, Israel, in November 1986, where I worked for Iscar until the Gulf War (1990–91) when I was faced with the upheaval of divorce.

In December 1992, I was invited to establish a new community in Northwood, where I stayed until the end of 1994 when I accepted a call to be the rabbi of Central Synagogue in January 1995. Here I met some wonderful people who responded to the challenge of reinvigorating the community and made this chapter of my life most satisfying and meaningful. The Central community were supportive of my Holocaust educational projects, especially the one-day trips to Auschwitz that I pioneered in 1998.

There were visits to other parts of Poland, Lithuania, Ukraine and Belarus, where I visited with my Uncle Morris in 2000 and found the 'home' of our Marcus grandparents in Zachowicze Gas (Street), Mir. I also managed to visit Baranowitz and saw where the Grawitsky's house stood in Slonim.

In 2014, I was knighted by the Polish president and in 2015 honoured with an MBE for my contribution to Holocaust education.

Although the recent passing of my mom (or 'Bobbe', as she was affectionately known) has left a vacuum in our family's lives, my greatest joy and satisfaction are my daughters – Lieba, Aviviya, Ora, Gabi and Eliana – along with Matan, Yoni, Ohad, Trevor and my thirteen grandchildren: Yair, Benaya, Amitai, Lia, Yael, Naveh, Noemie, Yochai, Ari, Eithan, Hillel, Tiago and Imri.

With gratitude to the Almighty.
הודו לַה' כִּי־טוֹב
London, October 2018 5779

A Man on a Mission: Rabbi Barry Marcus Reconnects Tens of Thousands with a Lost World

Rabbi Barry Marcus MBE in conversation with Rabbi Daniel Epstein about his motivation and passion for Holocaust education. (Article printed in the *Koren Machzor* for Yom Ha'Atzmaut and Yom Yerushalayim 2018.)

That was my house. It was very rabbinic. It was as if someone had transported a little piece of Lita (Lithuania) and relocated it to Cape Town.

Rabbi Barry Marcus of the Central Synagogue, Great Portland Street, London, may have been born in South Africa, but the world which he inhabited was suffused with the sounds, the smells, the language and a culture that, by the time he was born in the 1950s, no longer existed in its natural environment.

In this humble observation about displacement, lay the key to unlocking the passion and the innate need to communicate to tens of thousands about the lost Jewish world in Poland that would come to define a quarter-century of Rabbi Marcus' work.

* * * * * * *

Our story begins with Rabbi Shlomo David Grawitzky. Rabbi Grawitzky studied with some of the most respected and learned Rabbis of his generation. He was a student of the Chafetz Chaim – Rabbi Israel Meir Kagan – and his study partner ('*chavruta*') in Yeshiva in Ponevezh was the 'Ponevezher Rov', Rabbi Yosef Shlomo Kahaneman. He received his semichah from Rabbi Avraham Tzvi Kamai, the Mir 'Stodt Rov' (city Rabbi).

Living and working in Slonim, Poland (now Belarus), Rabbi Grawitzky part-owned a wood factory that specialised in making matches. His partner in the business was the Slonimer Rebbe, Rabbi Avraham Weinberg.

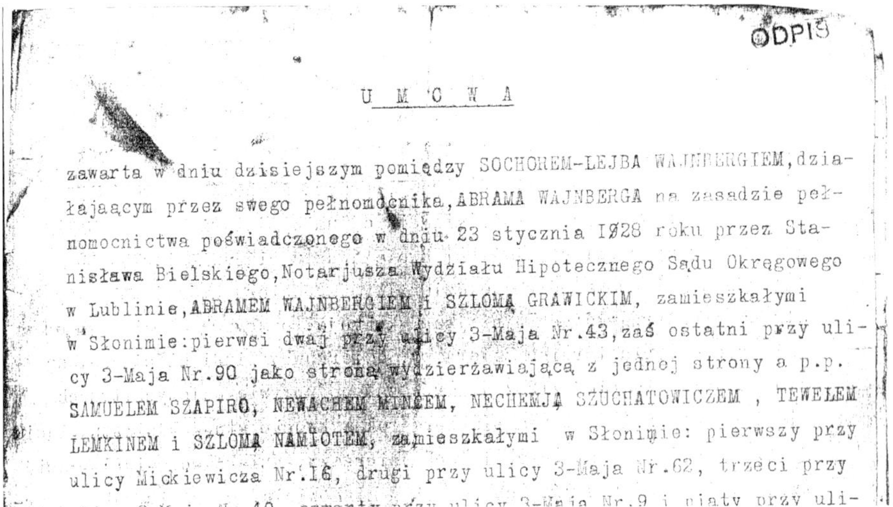

ODPIS

U M O W A

zawarta w dniu dzisiejszym pomiędzy SOCHOREM-LEJBA WAJNBERGIEM, działającym przez swego pełnomocnika, ABRAMA WAJNBERGA na zasadzie pełnomocnictwa poświadczonego w dniu 23 stycznia 1928 roku przez Stanisława Bielskiego, Notarjusza Wydziału Hipotecznego Sądu Okręgowego w Lublinie, ABRAMEM WAJNBERGIEM i SZLOMĄ GRAWICKIM, zamieszkałymi w Słonimie: pierwsi dwaj przy ulicy 3-Maja Nr.43, zaś ostatni przy ulicy 3-Maja Nr.90 jako stroną wydzierżawiającą z jednej strony a p.p. SAMUELEM SZAPIRO, NEWACHEM MINCEM, NECHEMJĄ SZUCHATOWICZEM, TEWELEM LEMKINEM i SZLOMĄ NAMIOTEM, zamieszkałymi w Słonimie: pierwszy przy ulicy Mickiewicza Nr.16, drugi przy ulicy 3-Maja Nr.62, trzeci przy ulicy 3-Maja Nr.9 i piąty przy uli-

Commercial contract for the match factory, showing [Rabbi] Avraham Weinberg and [Rabbi] Shlomo Grawitsky as partners.

One evening, there was an arson attack and the wood factory was burned down. The perpetrators were found and apprehended. Rabbi Grawitsky went to court, won the case and the court instructed that the factory should be rebuilt.

Soon after the factory was rebuilt, it was burned down a second time. This time, the Slonimer Rebbe advised Rabbi Grawitzky that it was no longer safe in Poland. Rabbi Grawitzky followed many other Lithuanian and Polish Jews who were looking for a less oppressive and more economically fruitful life overseas, and he took his wife, Lieba, and their three children and boarded a boat, bound for Cape Town, South Africa.

Rabbi Grawitzky was supposed to collect funds in South Africa for the Slonim Yeshiva, but he was a hopeless collector. Too gentle and unassuming, the local Jewish population made him their rabbi in the Woodstock Synagogue on Argyle Street, Cape Town, but he only agreed on condition that he would not take a salary. He was appointed as a Dayan in the Cape Town Beth Din, but he made his living by working in a kosher meat factory, where he earned a very modest wage.

In the Polish town of Mir, Avraham Isaac Markielewicz worked as a tailor and was also experiencing economic hardship. He had been corresponding with a pen-pal in South Africa who told him that life was good there, and that he should consider coming.

Rabbi Shlomo Grawitsky (Saba Shlomo).

Avraham came home one day, left money on the table and told his wife and eight children that he was leaving Poland and travelling by boat to Cape Town, South Africa. He promised he would send money every month until he could afford to bring them all to South Africa to join him.

The year was 1929. Avraham Markielewicz and Rabbi Shlomo Grawitzky [pictured on the previous page] arrived in England separately, but subsequently left Southampton on the same boat, bound for Cape Town.

True enough, in May 1934, Avraham Marcus (who, by now, had changed his last name from Markielewicz) sent for his wife, who joined him accompanied by 7 of his 8 children. Their eldest son – Nochum Arye Leib – stayed in the Mir Yeshiva for two more years.

Nochum Arye Leib had first studied in Baranovitch Yeshiva with Rabbi Elchonon Wasserman and then, for many years, in the famed Yeshiva of Mir, with Rabbis who included the 'Roshei Yeshiva' (heads of the Yeshiva) Rabbi Yehudah Eliezer Finkel, Rabbi Chaim Zev Finkel and Rabbi Beinish Finkel. He also studied with Reb Chaim Shmuelvitz; all personalities of international renown in the Torah world.

In 1936, the Mir Yeshiva had to move to the city of Vilna in Lithuania, as Poland had become too dangerous, and Nochum Arye Leib rejoined his family in South Africa, by which time he had already received Semicha from Reb Yehuda Leib Fajn.

Speaking Russian, Polish, Yiddish and Hebrew, Avraham Marcus didn't know what to do with his son Nochum, but he remembered Rabbi Grawitzky from the boat trip and he took his son to meet Rabbi Grawitzky.

Rabbi Nochum Marcus and Rabbi Shlomo Grawitzky became Talmud study partners ('*chavruta*') despite the significant age gap and, soon enough, Rabbi Nochum Marcus was introduced to Rabbi Grawitzky's daughter, Esther. They subsequently married each other and had four children, including a son; Barry.

'So that is where I come from,' reminisced Rabbi Marcus, 'but not just geographically. I still sometimes think in Yiddish because these were the melodies and the words and the names of the places that I heard as a child: Slonim, Baranovitch, Ponevezh, Mir. These became part of the soundtrack of my life and this was the world in which I grew up.'

'The heads of the Ponevezh and Mir yeshivas, when they came to stay in Cape Town, stayed in my house as this was one of the only places they felt comfortable. So this world never faded for me.'

Barry Marcus travelled to Israel to study at the Ponevezh Yeshiva, and his brother went to Mir, in deference to the two giants of the Torah world whose presence in their lives had been so profound in Cape Town. Rabbi Marcus received his semicha and returned to South Africa, ultimately becoming rabbi of the Waverley Synagogue community in Johannesburg, but he left after a shocking racist attack and moved to Israel.

Some years later, he moved to London, ending up at the Central Synagogue in London's West End.

Once settled in London, he observed that, compared to South Africa, a lot fewer Jews were visiting Israel and even fewer had a working understanding of the Holocaust. But he was told that Anglo Jewry was very well informed about the Holocaust and that there was nothing to worry about. This tension continued for a number of months.

Monday September 14 1981 THE CITIZEN

Anti-semitic spray-painter strikes

A large, black anti-semitic Nazi slogan spray-painted on the garden wall of Rabbi Barry Marcus' house in Waverley, Johannesburg.

Rabbi fears for the safety of his wife and children

A SLOGAN identical to those painted on homes and properties of Jews in Nazi Germany, was spray-painted on the garden-wall of a Johannesburg rabbi's house early on Saturday morning.

Rabbi Barry Marcus, whose house adjoins the Waverley Synagogue, said he could not understand why his house had been singled out.

"Anyone would think the schul would be a more obvious target. This attack has made me very uneasy as I have small children," he said.

"It's no comfort to know it was the work of a very sick mind. Anti-semitism is the oldest disease in the world, but that doesn't make one feel better about it."

Rabbi Marcus and his wife, Angela, saw the slogan, "Joden verboden" and the swastikas as they walked to synagogue on Saturday morning, the Jewish sabbath.

Mrs Marcus told The Citizen she was very worried about the implications of the attack. "It's my house that was picked out — nobody else's. I'm very worried for the chilren's sake."

Rabbi Marcus said the attack was one of cowardice. "There has been an upsurge of anti-semitism and these people, with their unfounded hatred towards others, are becoming bolder in their cowardice."

It is ironic that Rabbi Marcus' house was selected for the attack. He founded and runs a crisis clinic for people of all religious beliefs at the Waverley Synagogue.

So in late 1995, he conducted an experiment. Honorary officers from various synagogues were asked to bring their representative youth leaders on a Sunday morning to a basic introduction seminar on the subject of the Holocaust. Rabbi Marcus challenged that if by the end of the Sunday morning session he could see that they knew their material and were familiar with Holocaust education and history, he would drop the subject and not talk about it again.

Rabbi Marcus wrote down the names of some of the concentration camps from Nazi Europe on a flipchart. Knowing the obsession that British people have with football, he added some well-known Premier League footballers into the list, just to make it interesting.

As they were reading through the list, the word 'Majdanek' appeared. At that point, one of the youth leaders said, 'Who does he play for?'

In 1996, Marcus, along with Rabbi Y Roll and Rabbi R Simon, managed to convince 18 people from the UK to join the March of the Living – a solidarity march through Auschwitz-Birkenau that takes place each year just after Passover on Israel's Holocaust Remembrance Day.

Each country would march according to the size of their delegation under the each country's respective flag, with the largest delegations marching first and the smallest national representations marching at the back.

The UK was the smallest group, behind countries including Greece, Paraguay and Colombia!

'That was the turning point for me,' recalls Marcus. 'It was a real failure! I knew that in terms of the lifestyle in the UK, to ask people to give up 3–5 days for Holocaust education would not be successful. It would have to be a shorter trip. What if it could be done in one day?'

At that stage, all admitted to Rabbi Marcus that something needed to be done to improve Holocaust education in the UK, so he began thinking about a worthwhile programme that would effectively introduce the youth to the Holocaust.

With the fall of the Berlin Wall came the demise of Communism and Rabbi Marcus saw an opportunity to enable people to easily cross the precious 21 miles of English Channel that separated England from the horrors of Nazi-occupied Europe. He decided to privately charter a 240-seater plane and take people to see Poland for themselves.

In late 1997, starting with word of mouth recommendations, within a few days, 240 people had signed up and, with just his secretary and him handling all of the travel arrangements and bookings, they flew to Krakow Airport.

'It was the beginning of using near "shock tactics" to try to shake people up,' says Marcus. 'We needed them to understand what they would be giving up in terms of all of their history and Jewish heritage, simply because they did not appreciate what we had and, most importantly, all that they could lose by not maintaining their traditions.'

Marcus continued, 'What if I could get you up very early in the morning, take you to Poland and have you back in your own bed that same night?'

He tried it, and it worked.

'It was a radical idea, but some Holocaust survivors were irate. How could I cheapen their entire experience of years of suffering and hardship, and reduce it to a single day; actually just 10 hours in Poland?! They thought I was being disrespectful.

That was a very hard part of the project for me. So I decided to take a few survivors with me on one of the early one-day trips. Almost all of them realised what I was trying to do, and they supported it from then onwards.'

Marcus ran many similar one-day trips and filled the planes every time. It was hard work with lots of challenges along the way, including one travel company that went bankrupt during preparations, but they managed to make it a successful project.

In late 1998, after completing about 15 trips, Barry Marcus was approached by Janice Lopatkin who was, at the time, CEO of the Holocaust Educational Trust ('HET'). The HET was a lobbying group, working in the British Parliament and highlighting incidents of antisemitism.

'They wanted to broaden their scope and so we started working together. In order that it would not feel like just another "school trip", we encouraged people to start writing about their experiences in Poland and send them to me.'

People sent poems and prose and pictures that had been inspired by their trips to Auschwitz and other places in Poland, and these literary pieces were turned into books of modern reactions to the Holocaust.

At first, the narratives described by the Polish tour guides at places such as Auschwitz-Birkenau was very much about the Polish suffering during the Holocaust. However, over the years, the HET and Rabbi Marcus, along with other groups, insisted that the exhibits and information illustrate the significant Jewish aspect, and focus, of the camps' apparatus.

'It was only relatively recently, in the last 15 years, that Hebrew was added to the explanatory signs in and around Auschwitz,' Marcus remarked.

A lot of the Hebrew signage and research was down to the work of Professor Jonathan Webber, currently Professor of European Judaism and

European Jews at the Institute of European Studies of the Jagiellonian University in Poland, who was assisted by Chris Schwartz, an award-winning non-Jewish photographer from Bristol.

Chris was assigned to the project as a simple business assignment. Early on in the project, he found out that his father was Jewish, and became totally immersed in the project from that point on.

He moved to Krakow and embarked on a lifetime endeavour to capture as much history of lost Jewish Poland through his lens as he could, collating his images into what is now the Galicia Jewish Museum, for which Rabbi Marcus was instrumental in sourcing funding for its creation and maintenance.

The Polish government built a museum in Warsaw that is a testament to how Jews and Poles lived together in Poland for 800 years, but the Galicia Jewish Museum is the most comprehensive pictorial collection of lost Jewish communities from Poland.

Rabbi Marcus looks back on this period with pride. 'People of unbelievable dedication and inspiration were involved in the project. Andrew Dismore, MP for Hendon, joined me for one of the early trips in 1999. He subsequently stood up in Parliament and helped to table the motion for a Holocaust Memorial Day in the UK.'

On 10 June 1999, Andrew Dismore MP asked Prime Minister Tony Blair about the creation of special memorial day in the UK to commemorate the atrocities of the Holocaust. In reply, Tony Blair also referred to the ethnic cleansing that was being witnessed in the Kosovo War at that time and said: 'I am determined to ensure that the horrendous crimes against humanity committed during the Holocaust are never forgotten. The ethnic cleansing and killing that has taken place in Europe in recent weeks are a stark example of the need for vigilance.'

So, in addition to private trips for the Jewish community, from doing just two HET trips a year in 1998 – one for students and one for teachers – government funding was received and the project grew to its current capacity of 18 trips each year: over 4,000 students a year, with their educators.

'I never thought I would have the chance to expose this important work, not just to the UK Jewish population about their history, but to explain to the wider British public about the importance of Holocaust Studies, so that the next generation will understand. When statements are made in the public arena by individuals or organisations that are anti-Semitic, they should recognise them and know that they are wrong and speak out against this type of vilification, Holocaust denial, dilution of the facts and other misinformation.'

'And it makes an impact,' he continues. 'As I know from letters I receive, many students have even changed their higher educational direction. In some cases, students have changed university degrees or adjusted elective choices to take more of an interest in history, sociology, psychology and other fields that had been brought into sharper focus as a result of the emotional impact of their visit to Poland.'

It is a delicate project, largely dependent on government funding at this level of activity, but he hopes that it will continue for the foreseeable future.

'This project can be used to help people to understand and empathise with the inherent dangers of instability that Europe is increasingly experiencing in recent times, and having an appreciation of the behaviours that led to the Holocaust may help to ensure that this will never happen again.'

In 2014 at the Polish Embassy in London, Barry Marcus was awarded the Knight's Cross of the Order of Merit of the Republic of Poland for Holocaust Education and for fostering dialogue and building bridges with Poland.

He was awarded an MBE in the 2015 New Year's Honours for services to Holocaust Education.

* * * * * * *

Pictured from left: grandfather Avraham Marcus, Rabbi Barry Marcus and father Rabbi Nochum Arye Leib Marcus at Rabbi Barry's bar mitzvah, Cape Town, 1962.

'I feel very privileged for the type of upbringing I had, with the involvement of so many giants of Torah as part and parcel of my everyday life as a child and as a teenager.

Looking back on my childhood in South Africa, I remember that many of my friends would be driven to school by their chauffeurs or in their own expensive cars. I asked my father why we were living such a spartan existence, as it was not easy for me as a teenager to be so different from them.

My father pulled a well-worn Hebrew Bible off the shelf from years of loving and constant use and, holding it out for me to see, said: "*Mein teier kind; oib ich hobt dos, hobt ich alles*" – my darling child, if I have this, I have everything!'

Rabbi Marcus pauses for a second, staring past me, out into that lost world again, 'I didn't understand what he meant then, but I understand it now.'

A one-to-one trek, top of Mount Sinai, 1995.

Left to right: Stanley Lewis, Eric Charles and Rabbi Marcus, 1996.

Lord Mayor of Westminster, the arboricultural officer Paul Akers of Westminster City Council, councillors of the ward, together with members of the Central Synagogue Friendship Club, Tu Bi'Shvat, 1998.

Children's Chanukah party, 1998.

Rabbi Marcus with his uncle Morris after donating two Sifrei Torah to the emerging community in Minsk, 2000.

Above: Danny Elkanati, managing director of State of Israel Bonds, presents a Salvador Dali Menorah to Rabbi Marcus for Central Synagogue, 2002.

Left: The 60th anniversary of the liberation of Bergen Belsen – by the memorial for Anne and Margot Frank, 2005.

Right: The 60th anniversary of the liberation of Bergen Belsen, 2005.

Below: A memorial service for 7/7, Trafalgar Square, 2005.

Above: Holocaust Memorial Day football match at Upton Park. An all-party parliamentary team vs an XI of survivors' children and grandchildren team assembled by the Holocaust Educational Trust, 2005.

Below: Rabbi Marcus with Judge Bach (of the Eichmann Trial), 2010.

Above: Rabbi Marcus with Ambassador Ron Prosor, 2010.

Right: Purim morning, 2011.

Above: Rabbi Marcus with Henry Grunwald OBE QC, Yom HaShoah ceremony, Hyde Park, 2011.

Below: Yom HaShoah ceremony with Rabbi Lord Sacks, Rabbi Marcus and Lord Michael Howard, 2011.

Above: Yom HaShoah ceremony, Hyde Park, 2011.

Below: Addressing school groups in the Children's Synagogue, 2013.

At the Polish Embassy speaking about 'The Way Forward in Polish-Jewish Relations' at the 'History of the Kowalski's' film screening, 2013.

Above: Campaign for Youth Social Action at Clarence House with His Royal Highness Prince Charles, 2013.

Right: Lag B'Omer barbecue at Central, 2014.

Left: Speaking at the Jan Karski Holocaust Memorial event, 2014.

Below: Rabbi Marcus and Israeli Ambassador Daniel Taub at the Polish Embassy, 2014.

Above: Polish Ambassador Witold Sobków with Rabbi Marcus (and daughters Gabi, Aviviya, Eliana and Lieba), having been awarded the Knight's Cross of the Order of Merit of the Republic of Poland for Holocaust education and for fostering dialogue and building bridges with Poland, 2014.

Below: Interfaith Coexist event, 2015.

Left, below and opposite: Rabbi Marcus receiving his MBE for services to Holocaust education at Buckingham Palace from His Royal Highness Prince Charles, 2015. Seen below with his daughters, from left to right: Aviviya, Lieba, Eliana, Gabi and Ora.

Rabbi Marcus with Ashley Blaker, 2015.

Rabbi Marcus with Matt Lucas, 2015.

Belarus evening, 2017.

Right: Rabbi Marcus with Ephraim Zuroff, 2017.

Below: Tel Aviv University Trust talk, 2017.

Above: Yom HaZikaron and Yom Ha'Atzmaut celebrations, 2018.

Below: Rabbi Marcus with Rabbi Joseph Dweck of the S&P Sephardi Community, 2018.

Photos from the House of Commons Reception Hosted by Michael Gove MP Held in Honour of Rabbi Marcus, 2018

Above: Rabbi Marcus with Gordon Hausmann, 2018.

Below: Rabbi Marcus with Michael Gove MP.

Above: Ambassador Mark Regev.

Below: Jeremy Hunt MP.

Right: Jeremy Hunt MP and Rabbi Andrew Shaw.

Below: From left to right: Eliana, Ora, Jeremy Hunt MP, Rabbi Marcus, Aviviya and Gabi.

Above: Michael Gove MP making a presentation to Rabbi Marcus.

Below: Rabbi Marcus with his five daughters, from left to right: Aviviya, Ora, Lieba, Eliana and Gabi.

Above: Left to right: Aviviya, Matan, Ora, Trevor, Lieba, Tiago, Rabbi Marcus, Yoni, Gabi, Yan and Eliana.

Below: Henry Grunwald (L) and Jacques Weisser (R) presenting Rabbi Marcus with a Lifespan Award at the Yom HaShoah ceremony in Hyde Park. This was made in recognition of his unique contribution to Holocaust education, commemoration and remembrance in the UK through his many years of service to the Jewish community, particularly with Yom HaShoah UK and Yad Vashem UK, 2019.

Articles in the United Synagogue *Daf Hashavua* Publication

Lech L'cha
7 November 1992
11 Cheshvan 5753

In the wake of the mass *Aliyah* to Israel from the former Soviet Union, Eastern Bloc countries and Ethiopia, Shabbat parashat *Lech L'cha* has recently, throughout Israel, been given the title of *Shabbat Aliyah*. On this Shabbat communities have been called upon to invite all new neighbouring immigrants to synagogue and home. This practical and commendable expression of hospitality is also an attempt at exposing the new immigrants to our traditions, for sadly, many of them, due to their enforced isolation, have little or no knowledge of things Jewish.

The choice of this week's Torah reading to highlight *Aliyah* is quite obvious, for our forefather Abraham in his journey from Haran to the promised land is seen as the precursor of modern day *Aliyah*.

The parallel between Abraham's epic journey and present day *Aliyah* is quite evident, but on closer scrutiny of Genesis Chapter 12 Verse 1, it becomes abundantly clear that we are not only dealing with a physical journey in the accepted sense.

The opening verse of *Lech L'cha* reads as follows: 'Now the Lord said unto Abram: "Get thee out thy country, and from thy kindred, and from thy father's house."'

The order in this verse of the words 'thy country ... thy kindred ... thy father's house' has attracted much attention from our Rabbis. If Abram was commanded to embark on a physical journey, the verse should have read instead 'get thee out of thy father's house, from thy kindred and from thy country' for when a person sets off on a physical journey, he first leaves his house, thereafter his city ('kindred') and lastly his country. The suggestion is that the reversal of the order is to indicate a different kind of journey.

The aim of the Lord's command to Abram was not only as Rashi points out, to remove him from the negative influence of his surroundings, but ultimately to, 'make of thee a great nation' as we read in Chapter 12 Verse 2. In order to undergo this transformation, Abram had to embark not only on a physical journey, but more importantly, a spiritual journey. The reversal of the normal sequence was vital to achieve the set divine goal.

The Torah, in carefully recording the order as we read it, understands that if a person is to completely disassociate himself from his past, his surroundings and environment, the first and easiest thing one forgets is one's country. Thereafter one's recollections of one's city ('kindred') recede, but the most difficult memory to eradicate is that of one's father's house. It has often been remarked that one has difficulty in recalling what one did yesterday while childhood memories are vividly recollected.

Judaism understands that one's formative years are most critical, as is so aptly expressed by the oft quoted Talmudic saying: גירסא דינקותא – 'Lessons learned while young are not easily forgotten.' (Shabat 21)

We recognise that what one learns, what one gleans and what one is exposed to while young is indelibly inscribed in our very being and psyche.

A further comment emphasising the vital importance of the power and influence of education when young is expressed in the *Ethics of the Fathers* Chapter Four Mishna 20 – הלומד ילד – 'One who learns in one's youth, to what is such a person comparable? – To ink written on fresh paper.'

We live in an age when all too many of our brethren are travelling – often sadly journeying away from their tradition and roots, and this of course gives cause for much concern. There is much discussion of late on this subject, also concerning solutions to reverse this trend. Education in Jewish terms is not only the responsibility of our educators and teachers. It is to be, if successful, a combined and complementary effort of both home and school. The opening words of our sidra indicate in no uncertain terms how critical the influence of our homes is.

Abram's journey of old is a challenge to us to make our homes bastions of our heritage in the face of the present day siege on our people's belief and values, and to etch in ourselves and our offspring an immutable commitment to our faith and its future.

Vayera – Negotiation
2 November 1996
20 Cheshvan 5757

While attending a Harvard Business School course some years ago, I recall the professor remarking that the success of negotiation lay in the ability of the negotiators to remove ego from nEGOtiating. I respectfully pointed out to the lecturer that there was already a precedent for doing precisely that, and more, in the early chapters of Bereshit. I was naturally referring to Abraham's famous 'conference' with the Almighty in Bereshit Chapter 18 Verses 15–33, with regard to the fate of Sodom and Gomorrah.

It may be true that much of life is an ongoing protracted series of negotiations other than the obvious examples from the world of commerce; parents negotiate with children, teachers with pupils, employers with employees and so on. Whereas most negotiations are in the main motivated by self-interest and self-serving, in today's Sidra, Vayera, we are exposed to negotiations where the motivation is anything but self-interest.

Abraham's deliberations with the Almighty are motivated by his keen sense of justice and virtue. The fact that the Almighty shares with Abraham his intention to destroy Sodom is precisely because the Almighty recognised that Abraham's sense of justice and kindness would be outraged if he would not have informed him of his plans. Ramban, Sforno and Alsheich all echo in their respective comments Abraham's concern for justice. That Abraham is imbued with a passion for justice and righteousness is further evidenced by possibly one of the most stirring and noble verses in the Torah – in his plea to the Almighty – Chapter 18:25.

'Far be it from Thee to do this thing to slay the righteous with the wicked, so that the righteous should be as the wicked. Far be it from Thee – shall not the Judge of the whole earth do justice?'

What is remarkable about Abraham's plea to save Sodom is that he does not mention his nephew Lot. Abraham's driving interest is that justice should be done. In doing so Abraham teaches us an invaluable lesson. Our sense of justice should not only be stirred when we as people are affected but also when an injustice is perpetrated no matter against whom. Abraham's imploring of the Almighty is all the more admirable, as even though Sodom and Gomorrah were infamous for their depravity and evil, Abraham was nevertheless not influenced by this and his desire for justice was no less genuine.

Abraham shows himself to be a truly righteous man in that he deplores possible injustice (against all of the inhabitants of Sodom) not because he himself or his family (Lot) may suffer but simply because a possible injustice may be carried out.

A comment by Sforno on Jacob's confrontation with the shepherds at the well (Bereshit Chapter 29:7) is the most appropriate with regard to Abraham's reaction to the news of the impending destruction of Sodom.

'The truly righteous man despises injustice against others.'

Abraham's imploring of the Almighty to reconsider on behalf of 50, 45, etc., is in stark contrast to Noah's silence when the Almighty informed him of his intention to destroy the world. We hear no passionate pleas from Noah. This is precisely why we are known as *Zera Avraham*, 'Seed of Abraham', and not *Zera Noah*, 'Seed of Noah'.

This very thought is corroborated by the Almighty's statement in Chapter 19:19 as to why he is sharing his plans with Abraham.

'For I have known him, because he commands his children and his household after him, that they may keep the way of the Lord to do righteousness and justice.'

All too often on both personal and communal levels, and also with regard to Israel, we react passionately only when injustices are aimed or perpetrated against us, but very rarely do we react with the same verve when injustice is perpetrated against others. We have sadly strayed from Abraham's lofty and dignified example of righteousness and justice and have, I believe, therefore lost much credibility as a people.

Abraham in his mediation with the Almighty concerning the fate of Sodom challenges us to re-establish ourselves as his true descendants by raising our voices and by taking active steps to always prevent injustice and not only when we are affected or threatened.

Mattot-Masei – Ownership of Land
2 August 1997
28 Tammuz 5757

In the concluding chapters of the book of Bamidbar which we read today we find what is virtually the last historical record in the Torah of the children of Israel in the wilderness.

In the lengthy but staccato like opening chapter of Massei (Ch. 33) we are almost invited to relive the wanderings of the children of Israel through the oft-repeated refrain '*Vayisu* ... *Vayachnu*' 'And they journeyed ... and they camped...' Then our weary ancestors, encamped on the shores of the Jordan, are told, '*Vehorashtem et Ha'aretz Vishavtem Bah*' – 'And you shall inherit the land and dwell therein' (33:53). One can imagine the relief of our people on being told that the hardships, trials and tribulations that they had endured were now approaching their end and that from the plains of Moab they could actually see their new permanent home.

As if to give the fatigued travellers a further sense of security, following the promise of '*Vehorashtem*' – 'And you shall inherit', the entire next chapter – Chapter 34 – records in detail the borders of the new land.

The subject of Israel's borders seems never to leave the front pages of the news. It would appear that from the earliest times, borders and boundaries have, and sadly continue, to be a source of conflict, strife and disagreement on international, national and individual levels.

We are educated to expect animals to be vigorously 'territorial' but there often seems to be little difference between the animal kingdom and man.

The purpose of delineating the borders of Israel in Chapter 34 elicits a remarkable and lofty comment from Rashi. His view is that the borders are mentioned not as an attempt to inculcate a sense of being 'territorial' but because of *Mitzvot Hanohagot Ba'aretz* the many commandments that are applicable only in the land of Israel, such as *Shemitah*, *Yovel*, *Orlah*, etc.

The borders are mentioned simply to assist in knowing the physical limits where certain divine commandments are to be observed.

The comment of Rashi where he sees marking of borders simply as 'religious aids' is difficult to reconcile with his earlier comment on 33:53 '*Vehorashtem*' – 'And you shall inherit' here Rashi says '*Vehorashtem ota miyoshveha – V'az veyshavtem ba Tuchlu L'Hitkayem ba V'im Lav Lo*

Tuchlu Lehitkayem' – 'Only if you clear the land of its former inhabitants will you be able to maintain yourself in the land, but not otherwise.'

Rashi is primarily concerned with their act of attaining ownership of the land and taking whatever steps to acquire.

In stark contrast is the comment of Ramban who states on the same 33:53 '*Al Da'ati zu Mitzvat Aseh Hi Yetzaveh Sheyeishvu Ba'aretz Vayarshu Otah, Ki, Hi Nitnah Lahem*' – 'According to my opinion this injunction (you shall inherit) is a divine positive commandment that they (the children of Israel) should dwell in the land and inhabit it for He (The Almighty) gave it to them.'

As opposed to his comment on 34:2 with regard to the borders of Israel here (33:53) Rashi posits a pragmatic view that our people could not flourish in the land as long as its former inhabitants still occupy it. His view is quite plain, namely that ownership (of Israel) has validity only when the title to its land cannot be contested by possession of other inhabitants.

Ramban on the other hand takes a more mystical view – possession is the paramount consideration – establishing a foothold in Jerusalem, a *Yeshivah* in Yavneh, a colony in Safed, etc. will certify our title to the land. Possession in his view is a *Mitzvat Aseh* – a positive commandment divinely sanctioned.

Hence Ramban travelled to Israel and encouraged others to follow his example. It is interesting to note the great importance our sages attached to living in Israel, and the prohibition against leaving it is derived from the self-same verse. Rashi focuses on the word '*Vehorashtem* – and you will inherit,' Ramban '*Veeshavtem* – and you shall dwell.'

The difference of views between Rashi and Ramban are not merely semantic but expresses the gap between the major political forces in Israel and the Diaspora and very often the rationale for exerting political pressure on Israel both from within and without.

Ownership and possession of Israel is today a much debated issue. The differences with which Israel is viewed is also expressed in a most illuminating *Gemara* – *Baba Batra* 117, commenting on Chapter 22:54 '*Vehitnachaltem Et Ha'Aretz* – and you shall divide the land'. The Talmud records two opinions – one that the land was divided and given to '*Yotzei Mitzraim*' i.e. those who departed from Egypt, and the second that the land was given to '*Boei Ha'aretz* – those who settled in the land'.

In today's terminology these two different opinions would be synonymous with the opposing views of the Zionist and Non-Zionist camps also referred to as Charedi and Secular camps. This growing divide in Israel is most disturbing. The Talmud concludes that the Halacha is that the land was given to both '*Yotzei Mitzraim*' and '*Boei Ha'aretz*'.

We have to appreciate that Torah and Israel are the two greatest genuine possessions of the Jewish people and that the two are inextricably intertwined. An understanding of the above would surely halt the unnecessary divisiveness that weakens and undermines Israel and world Jewry.

Devarim – Vision
1 August 1998
9 Av 5758

Today's sidra of *Devarim* is always read before Tisha B'Av. This year is no different even though today is the ninth of Av, as other than Yom Kippur, fast days that may fall on Shabbat are either postponed (*nidcheh*) or brought forward (*Mukdam*).

The Haftarah this Shabbat is the last of the '3 prophecies of rebuke' – (*shloshah D'Puranita*) read between the fast of 17th Tammuz and Tisha B'Av. Today is known as *Shabbat Chazon* (literally the Shabbat of Vision) taking its name from the opening word of the Haftarah (Isaiah Chapter 1) in which the prophet Isaiah shares his vision of Israel of old.

The prophet focuses on what he perceives to be the underlying cause for the destruction of our Temple, culminating in our exile. In a poetic yet forceful way the prophet expresses some uncompromising home truths – '*yadah shor koneihu v'chamor eivus ba'lav Yisrael lo yadah*' – 'an ox knows its master but Israel does not'. (Isaiah 1:3)

In a similar vein in a comment on the opening verse of the Book of Devarim – 'These are the words which Moses spoke,' the Commentary known as Sifrei asks somewhat incredulously but rhetorically if these were the only words that Moses spoke. The Sifrei continues to explain that these 'words which Moses spoke' were words of reproof and rebuke. When I read the above comment and hear the mournful *Eichah* (Lamentations) melody in which today's Haftarah is sung, I often wonder what Isaiah would say if he were alive on today's world stage. Would he be pleased with what he sees and compliment us or would his shame and embarrassment trigger a tirade of rebuke on us?

Aside from the fact that he would probably need a spin doctor and a vast public relations and media circus to accompany him, I suspect Isaiah would sadly not be taken aback by what he may observe. His words to today's 'Officers of Sodom and Gemorrah' (Isaiah 1:10) may possibly have to undergo some cosmetic changes but the message I suspect would be unchanged. He may well be surprised by high levels of anxiety that seem to beset Jewish communities here and elsewhere, but that may be explained away as post-Holocaust trauma.

The incessant bickering and petty arguments may on the other hand be a malady familiar to him, as also the obvious loss of focus of the supposedly *Am Kadosh* – Holy Nation. He would also probably find the petty bureaucratic nonsense that so many seem to be embroiled in, coupled with the seemingly insatiable craving for honour and acknowledgement (particularly from non-Jews) and the seeking of power mildly amusing but familiar.

Isaiah may well be impressed by the amazing powers of retention and memory enabling the average young Jewish boy to reel off by rote the names of entire football teams, but he may well be saddened on asking the same average youngster as to who Rambam is, for the retort will more often than not be 'for whom does he play?'

One of the better known recorded incidents in the Torah is the interaction of the snake with Eve. The Torah records '*Al g'choncha teileich*' 'on your belly you shall walk' (Bereshit 1:1). From the verse is deduced, that prior to its punishment, the snake walked in an upright position. Many have questioned the suitability of the punishment; for at first glance it may not even appear to be a punishment. On the contrary, the snake has to expend little energy on finding sustenance – being on 'ground level' makes his food source readily available. I once heard from my dear father and teacher of blessed memory, in the name of his illustrious Mashgiach, Rabbi Yerucham L'vovitch of the famous Yeshiva of Mir, that even though the punishment meted out may initially not appear to be appropriate, the snake's punishment in being doomed to crawl on its belly is that it could no longer lift his head and look heavenwards.

The comment comes to mind when I see so many in places of leadership (both Rabbinic and lay) inevitably looking down and behind, rarely ahead, and almost never heavenwards. This all too prevalent approach is not indigenous to our community but is sadly widespread and so succinctly summarised in a comment with regard to certain inappropriate practices on fast days (Shulchan Aruch Chapter 121) – *Tafsu et hatefel ve'hinichu, et haikar* – they adhere to the unimportant and marginal, and overlook the principle issue.

I recently led two one-day trips to Auschwitz with some 500 people from diverse backgrounds covering a wide spectrum of our community, I was quite overwhelmed by the size of the groups wanting to visit Auschwitz but more so by the reaction of both young and old. Many were visibly shaken by the experience.

We probably need an Isaiah to administer some kind of an electric shock to us to shake us out of our inertia, allowing us to see things with clarity of vision, motivating us to channel our energy in a more positive and constructive manner.

Above all we need to rediscover the vision and courage to make Judaism a sincere experience!

Shavuot – Megillat Ruth – The Unlikely Convert

21 May 1999
6 Sivan 5759

The connection between Shavuot and *Megillat Ruth* is threefold. Firstly, Shavuot is also known as *Chag Hakatzir* – the Festival of the Harvest; *Megillat Ruth* offers us an insight into agriculture and harvest in biblical times. Secondly, Shavuot is further known as *Z'man Matan Torateinu* – the season of the Giving of the Torah. Ruth's acceptance and attachment to Torah is central to the Scroll. Thirdly, according to our tradition, King David was born and died on Shavuot and Ruth was David's great grandmother.

Megillat Ruth, I suspect, will always have a strong appeal because of its ability to touch our hearts. We can identify with Naomi and Ruth as the drama of their lives unfolds, and we are stirred by the sublime kindness and care displayed by Boaz. All of the above is already well documented, researched and commented on. I would, however, like to focus on the issue of conversion against the backdrop of Ruth, one of our most famous 'converts'.

Israel has become the battlefield for the legitimising of conversions by those who operate outside the parameters of Halachah. It is of course interesting to note the paltry and insignificant number of so called 'converts' who actually have a genuine interest in, and who make, Aliyah – some of the more publicised cases have of course all returned to their countries of origin; all this contrary to the impression created that this is an issue affecting thousands of so-called converts impatiently waiting to accept Torah and willing to do anything to embrace Judaism. Through vigorous use of the media and in co-operation with other self-denigrating elements in Israeli society, the general Jewish public has been sorely misled. All of the above is really part of a different agenda and it is not about conversion or the issue of who is a Jew – but who is a Rabbi!

Many a Rabbi is asked why conversion is made so difficult; why cannot it be made as simple as in the case of Jethro or Ruth? Without challenging whether Ruth's (or Jethro's) conversion was in fact made easy, and not withstanding our obligation to treat the '*Ger*' (convert) with understanding as recorded in the Talmud – *Sanhedrin 94a*, and Rashi on Shemot 18:9 '*De'amrei Inshei, Giyuta...*' 'Speak not disparagingly about a proselyte,' there are two distinct types of prospective converts – one a convert of conviction and the other a convert of convenience.

Few congregational Rabbis today are faced with the former, many with the latter. In dealing with conversion, our community is particularly fortunate in that there is a central yet independent Beth Din dealing with conversion, unlike the USA where individual Rabbis are called upon to deal with prospective members of their own community. This method brings with it a host of problems not least of all the 'legitimacy' of the Rabbi involved, his objectivity and other serious social problems and pressures within the community.

Conversion is a highly emotive and complex subject – there are those who are stubbornly dismissive of the process believing that it is intrinsically an impossibility and therefore a 'non-starter'. Those of this opinion will argue that since we are genetically, culturally, consciously, sub-consciously different, our values and attitudes are therefore divergent from other peoples. This point of view makes no distinction between converts of conviction or convenience. Others who are 'uncomfortable' with converts of convenience justify their reserve by referring to the statistic of so many such converts (of convenience) returning to their former status.

The diluting and changing of standards to accommodate conversions in general, and those of convenience in particular, is a serious malaise facing world Jewry and the rightful reluctance of authentic and responsible *Batei Din* to follow suit is to be applauded. The present climate is exacerbated by the fact that we already have enough problems of commitment and observance with our own born, Jews. Coupled with this attitude of caution towards converts is our desire not to appear evangelical, as the very thought of being a missionary is a total anathema. The argument that we need to be more accommodating with regard to conversion in order to bolster our falling numbers is of course fallacious. If those misguided organisations, the protagonists of this view, are to be believed, then why are we in fact in decline? All that has happened is that organisations have facilitated wholesale destruction and divisions effectively creating new and unnecessary barriers. The ramification of dubious conversions might not be seen or felt immediately but when the offspring get to a marriageable age, the problems begin to surface. (The same is sadly true when Jewish couples fail to obtain a *Get.*)

Once age-old Halachic requirements and regulations regarding status are tampered with, you effectively create a different people – as the word itself indicates; when you reform something you change it from its original form – it is a new and different creation.

Whatever opinion one may hold, all will agree as to the complex nature of conversion. I heard one of the best descriptions of the difficulties facing both the convert and Beth Din while involved with conversions at the Johannesburg Beth Din some years ago, when a colleague remarked that to effect a genuine and successful conversion you have to 'REWIRE' the person.

How many of us today can stand up and honestly like Ruth (Chapter 1:15) say 'Your G-d is my G-d' and really mean the G-d of Abraham, Isaac and Jacob? There is no need to change our beliefs or standards – the only conversion we need today is from apathy and indifference to genuine commitment, observance and pride.

Ruth is a constant source of inspiration to us – for in her case everything militated against her following Naomi. Yet she embraced Judaism unconditionally. Ruth challenges us to 'plug in' to authentic Judaism and effect changes in ourselves and not with our faith.

Tazria – Legislate or Educate?

8 April 2000
3 Nisan 5760

Uvayom Hashemini Yimol B'sar Orlato – 'And on the eighth day the flesh of his foreskin shall be circumcised'. (Vayikra 12:3)

Even though the mitzvah of *Brit Milah* (circumcision) is previously mentioned in Bereshit (17:10–14), from the repetition in this week's Torah reading we derive from the word UVAYOM (on the day) the practice to perform a Brit only during the daytime.

The practice of circumcision has recently been in the spotlight and the subject of much discussion. Not surprisingly, the producer of a recent biased and negative TV programme was ostensibly from amongst our own. This is, of course, sadly nothing new nor is the discussion by so-called 'experts' on this subject.

The Yalkut (early collection of Midrashic Literature, circa 12th century) records an exchange almost two thousand years ago between Rabbi Akiva and a Roman Officer who questioned the saintly Rabbi as to the purpose of *Brit Milah*.

Painful mitzvot

The fact that of all the mitzvot of the Torah many Jews generally choose to observe the most physically demanding and painful ones i.e. Yom Kippur and circumcision, is possibly an interesting subject for a more indepth psychological study which is not my intention or brief in this essay.

I do not know if there are any statistics available, but I am led to believe that the practice of the mitzvah of *Brit Milah* has the possible distinction of being one of the few mitzvot observed worldwide by even the least observant and committed amongst us. A point in case is modern day Israel.

Religion and politics

Despite the regrettable tension and polarisation in Israeli society, even the most indifferent of Jewish families will almost always automatically insist on their sons being circumcised. Yet when it comes to Shabbat observance (or Pesach) anyone who has lived in Israel or visited will know of the wholesale desecration of Shabbat in most major centres throughout the country. Why this anomaly? In Israel I suggest much is due to the unholy mix of *Dat U'Medina* – politics and religion. I strongly suspect that if, in their zealousness, the well meaning, but often misguided religious politicians were to introduce a law enforcing *Brit Milah* in Israel, it would suffer the same fate as the Shabbat and Pesach observance laws and invite resentment, hostility and rejection. I would challenge anyone in Israel to point to increased religious observance and commitment due to Knesset legislation. The law forbidding *chametz* on Pesach, for example, has simply created the bizarre phenomena of many Israelis travelling great distances to Arab shops and villages to eat bread. With regard to Shabbat, the sight of committed Jews demonstrating outside a cinema in Petach Tikva or elsewhere on a Friday night is indeed saddening and more distressing. Would not more have been achieved in maintaining the Jewish character? Would not the soul of Israel been better served if those demonstrating would simply have invited those in the cinema into their homes to experience the joys of a Shabbat meal and atmosphere?

We in the diaspora can learn from the failed Israeli experience where it is patently obvious that when it comes to faith and its observance the way forward is to educate, to motivate and not to legislate.

Joys of Judaism

It has been said that Judaism is often more 'caught than taught'. Frequently the frontal, formal approach invites the exact opposite desired effect. There is nothing wrong with Torah and its message – it is however ironic in an age of instant sophisticated and global communication that we have not found an effective way of transmitting the value, beauty and relevance of Torah.

Many unaffiliated Jews still see Judaism as forboding, austere and unwelcoming – an image we need collectively to shed if we are to win the hearts of the growing number of unaffiliated and disaffected. The increasing number of single people, divorcees, widows and widowers would also dearly like to feel part of the community. Their unease and discomfort, and that of others, needs to be addressed not through conferences or resolutions or meaningless speeches but through a concerted effort to open our hearts, our homes, our Synagogues and communities to all, and this is where our energy and resources should be focused. *D'racheha darchei Noam* – 'the ways of the Torah are pleasant' (Proverbs 3:18) – today with the wealth of technology available to us we have an ideal opportunity to demonstrate the joys of authentic Judaism, and by example to inspire those amongst us to retain and strengthen their links with our remarkable heritage.

Re'eh – To Which Synagogue Do You Belong?

18 August 2001
29 Av 5761

Today's Torah reading mentions the injunction to build a central '*Mishkan*' – sanctuary (Devarim 12). With a month to go to the High Holydays, it may be appropriate to reflect on our modern day 'Sanctuaries' against the backdrop of those of old.

The spiritual contribution and impact of the synagogue is immeasurable as, unlike the Temple, it was and is not bound to any particular place, but a portable home of the spirit.

This contribution is succinctly expressed by R. Travis Herford – 'In all their long history, the Jewish people have done scarcely anything more wonderful than to create the synagogue.' (*The Pharisees*, 1924)

Its functions

Over the centuries, the Synagogue became the fount of the Jewish spirit, a place where all Jews assembled for inspiration and strength, for thanksgiving and consolation, for solace and study, for prayer and moral regeneration. It was a *Bet Hatefillah* and a *Bet Hamidrash* – a 'house of prayer' and 'study'. It was also a *Bet Haknesset* – a 'house of assembly' where communal problems were discussed.

At times, the Synagogue even becomes a people's court – any Jew who felt that he had a just grievance against another had the right to hold back the reading of the Torah until he gained a public promise of a just and impartial hearing. This form of appealing for justice, which may appear strange to us, was fully understood by the worshippers in the synagogue of old. What value is there in the reading of the law if the congregation will tolerate an injustice?

This was the synagogue to which all Jews belonged and the spirit which permeated every phase of Jewish life. It was the spiritual, social and cultural reservoir and dynamo of the Jewish community.

Belonging to the synagogue did not mean for Jews through the centuries membership in a particular synagogue, determined by paying a stated amount of annual dues, as is the normal criterion of synagogue affiliation today.

Commitment

There is a fundamental difference, and in this difference we see the greatest and gravest challenge to the quality of Jewish life today and to our very survival as Jews. Not only do we have a large number of Jews unaffiliated with the synagogue in any sense of the word, but a great many of those who do consider themselves synagogue members, belong only in a superficial sense. Belonging to the synagogue means more than paying dues – it means primarily **commitment**.

When one's connection with the synagogue is only fiscal, then his or her relationship to it is simply like that of a stock-holder in a business corporation. The corporation belongs partly to him – he does not belong to the corporation. The historic relationship between the Jew and the synagogue was not that the Jew possessed the synagogue but rather the reverse. The synagogue possessed him; he was possessed by its spirit which guided, inspired and strengthened his life as a Jew.

It is no wonder many complain that they get little out of 'belonging to the synagogue'. The fact is that they do not belong to the synagogue – they want the synagogue to belong to them. They do not want to get much from the synagogue; they only give something to it, and what they give is not their hearts and minds but only some gold. While there is a record of gold making a calf, we do not know of a case where gold made a man.

Fortunately, we do have many congregants who belong to the synagogue in the historic sense and turn to it for sincere worship, for learning and for inspiration, seeking spiritual improvement in their own lives.

As I travel through Eastern Europe and visit the forlorn and empty synagogues, I am filled with sadness at the terrible loss of once vibrant communities. But I am equally grateful and humbled that we in the UK are privileged with the opportunity to regenerate Jewish life in freedom. Nevertheless, what is our relationship with our synagogue?

Reconnect

Do we regard it as something belonging to us, or do we belong to it? Is it another one of our possessions, or does it possess us? Are we merely giving it our dues, or are we willing to accept the duties and doctrines which it offers us? On the threshold of a new year, may we find the courage to answer these questions sincerely and the desire to re-connect to the fortress of our faith – the synagogue.

Yitro – Sidra Insights
2 February 2002
20 Shevat 5762

Even though one can understand the deep-rooted psychological and emotional need for affirmation and acknowledgement, I note with a touch of amusement the preoccupation bordering on obsession with honours, accolades and a variety of prizes that has given rise to what is today a global industry. In the UK most are already conditioned, while others are captivated by the traditional honours list published every year-end.

This is, however, no longer a once a year phenomenon. The worldwide plethora of honours lists in every walk of life is now not only common place – whether they are Oscars, Baftas, Man/Woman of the year etc., but they have also lost their original appeal, whilst others have lost any value or gravitas they may have previously enjoyed. (Note the recent furore over whether Bin Laden should be voted Man of the Year by a well-known American publication or the perverse award of the Nobel Peace Prize to Arafat.)

In view of the above, let us explore and examine why Jethro is given the signal honour of having a Sidra named after him – and not just any Sidra – but one that contains, arguably, the most momentous and defining event in our long and illustrious history – the revelation at Mount Sinai. This is all the more perplexing as there is no Sidra named after Biblical greats like Moses and Abraham. The Torah relates that when Jethro saw that Moses was exhausted in carrying out his duties, he said, '*lo tov hadavar*' – it is not wise for you to assume the burden all by yourself. Jethro advised Moses to delegate his responsibilities and lighten his load.

In our climate today of large corporations and conglomerates, Jethro's simple message is probably most obvious, but nevertheless valid and relevant. No person, no leader, however talented, can carry the burden alone. In the interests of efficiency and success, there needs to be a distribution of energy and skills. It is interesting to note that even though Jethro suggested to Moses that he select leaders who had four qualities – (Shemot 18:21) men of valour, G-d fearing people, men of truth and men who despise bribery, the Torah records that Moses only selected *anshei chayil* – men of valour, for they would presumably, as men of valour, have the courage to remain steadfast to their ideals and speak out when others choose to remain silent.

Our sages note that Jethro was rewarded for his insightful suggestion by having the letter '*vav*' added to his name, which was previously Yeter. The letter *vav* means 'and' or 'with' and is used in Hebrew as a conjunction called *vav hachibur* – the *vav* that combines or ties. Herein lies Jethro's legacy worthy of honour, for the *vav* teaches us the simple yet profound lesson that in combining, there is strength. Especially in view of recent and ongoing events in Israel and elsewhere, Jethro challenges us to reconnect to the Torah, and to each other.

The honour bestowed on Jethro of having a Sidra named after him is principally due to his unconditional acceptance of Judaism, which in a sense makes him the forerunner and ultimate 'Man of the Year' and 'Man of his Age'.

Tazria – Powers of Renewal

5 April 2008
29 Adar II 5768

Our Torah reading today introduces us to the concept of *Tzara'at* in its various forms. *Tzara'at* is often incorrectly translated as 'leprosy' but it is quite clear that this affliction, which seems to have been a common ailment in ancient times, was the physical manifestation of a spiritual illness and it was therefore the Cohanim (Priests) who played a pivotal role in the diagnosing and determining of its treatment.

There is the well-known suggestion made by our Sages of the connection between *Tzara'at* the affliction and *Metzora* the one affected by it. The word *Metzora* can be split into two – *Motzi Ra* i.e. he who spreads evil/slander. The clear inference is that due to an inability to control one's speech and the subsequent 'pollution of the mouth' one became vulnerable to contracting *Tzara'at.*

If we look at the word for the description of *Tzara'at* it is described as a *Nega* – a plague. If we simply reverse these 3 letters, we get the word *Oneg* meaning delight/pleasure.

Even though the concepts of *Oneg* and *Nega* are seemingly opposite, the correlation between them is worthy of some reflection.

Professionals in the area of Crisis Intervention point out that even in our lowest, darkest moments, we have the ability to find the strength to extract something positive from what may initially appear be a hopeless situation.

A similar thought is to be found in today's reading [from the 2nd Sefer] for *Parshat HaChodesh*, the last of the 4 special Shabbatot preceding Pesach, designed to remind us of our need to begin our preparation for the festival. The reading initially deals with the establishment of *Nissan* as the first month of the year. The Hebrew word for month is *Chodesh* which contains in it the word for new or to renew – *chadash*. We as a people have always found the ability, no matter what difficulties we have had to face, to renew our commitment to our faith and to find the resolve to successfully confront countless challenges. The establishment of the State of Israel, in the wake of the Shoah, in this, the 60th anniversary year, is an obvious example of the correlation between *Nega* and *Oneg*.

This past week, the community of Central Synagogue was privileged to mark the 50th Anniversary since the consecration of its present Synagogue, after the original one was bombed in 1941 and rebuilt after the war as an act of faith in the future. The Central, established in 1855, and the last remaining of the original 5 communities to constitute the United Synagogues in 1870, is an admirable example of our powers of renewal. We pay tribute to the vision and efforts of those members past and present who helped renew this community and to those who today help maintain it.

May the Almighty bless them along with all others who faithfully occupy themselves with the needs of all our communities.

VA'ETCHANAN – FROM WHERE WILL COMFORT COME?

1 August 2009
11 Av 5769

Every year during the three week period known as *Bein Hametzarim*, 'between the straits', beginning with the fast of Tammuz and culminating with Tisha b'Av, we try to relive our people's experience of persecution and exile. This is followed by *Shabbat Nachamu*, the Shabbat of Comfort. This name is taken from the well-known opening words of today's haftarah from the prophet Isaiah, *Nachamu, nachamu ami*, 'be comforted, be comforted, my people'.

This haftara and the next six are known as *Shiva deNechemta*, the seven [haftarot] of comfort, which, unlike most haftarot, do not reflect the subject of the weekly Torah-reading, but rather the period in our calendar. This is to offer some therapeutic consolation after the tragic events that we remember during the sad period of the Three Weeks.

We live in distinctly uncomfortable times – whether we reside in Sderot, Ashkelon, Nahariya, London, or Paris – or if we just happen to be visiting the Holocaust Museum in Washington. If you are not sure as to the levels of discomfort, ask our young, newly-arrived French men and women who have recently moved to London and who now attend our synagogues.

Our prophets of old promise consolation after destruction, exile and other great tragedies. Isaiah in today's *haftarah* refers to the revival of Israel and the return to Jerusalem. In these prophecies there is also reference to a return to G-d and reconciliation with the Almighty.

Our generation is certainly privileged to have witnessed the first part coming true in a glorious and miraculous fashion – almost daily – before our own eyes.

The question that is often posed is why Moses is not the harbinger of the ultimate *geulah* [redemption] and why is it Elijah. It is Elijah whom we invite on Seder night, or to a *Brit Milah* or to solve talmudical problems (*Teku*).

Rav Soleveitchik posits that it is not Elijah's life and personality that makes him the prophet of redemption, but the fact that in his lifetime G-d taught him a lesson which is necessary for all of us to assimilate both for present action and future redemption. This is the lesson of patience, the lesson that came with the vision in the cave – the *kol demamah daka*, 'the small silent voice' as described in I Kings Chapter 19.

We glean from here that you don't change people or situations overnight. Elijah learnt that through patience and love of your fellow man you can effect change, and it is this quality that makes him eminently suitable to be the harbinger of the final redemption.

Elijah challenges us to genuinely embrace patience and tolerance in order to make an impact on all our lives and thereby hopefully hasten the ultimate redemption and, in its wake, the comfort we all yearn for.

Shofetim – Of Judges and Gates
25 August 2012
7 Ellul 5772

It has been a year since the lives of countless individuals and communities were blighted by the riots in London, Manchester, Birmingham and elsewhere. Whilst buildings and businesses were still smouldering, various experts were paraded in the media, offering their theories and, in some cases, vindications. Their opinions flooded in almost at the same speed as the looters ransacked targeted stores in search of desired brand-name goods.

Although outrage and surprise were expressed, this was drowned out by the hasty and insipid attempts to find justification for the inexcusable behaviour of so many. In contrast, there was little by way of squarely placing the responsibility where it belonged – with the perpetrators. The lengths that some went to deny culpability and suggest extenuating circumstances in order to excuse the violent behaviour was disheartening and disappointing.

Such a response is certainly at odds with the Torah's perspective. At the end of Parashat Shofetim, we read (21:1–9) about the *Eglah Arufah* (beheaded heifer). If a dead body was found between two cities, a ceremony was held which included the elders of both adjoining cities declaring sorrow at the loss of life. The ceremony was designed to publicly express communal responsibility for the tragic crime committed. The leaders of the two cities closest to the corpse declared, 'Our hands have not spilled this blood' (21:7). The message was that although they may not have physically been involved with the murder, they did however bear a measure of responsibility. They could not react with indifference to a crime albeit committed beyond their own city limits. The Torah is stressing social accountability.

The opening verse of the sidra reads: 'Judges and officers **you** shall appoint at all your gates' (16:18). The Talmud (Shabbat 119) suggests that the specific use of 'you' in the singular is to encourage us to correct our own defects before judging others. In a similar vein, the Sefer HaYetzira (lit. the Book of Creation, an early esoteric text c. 2nd century BCE) offers an interesting comment on the last words of the same verse – 'at all your gates'. The 'gates' mentioned in the verse do not refer to a physical, tangible gate, rather to the gates of one's soul – one's eyes, mouth and ears. This is where policing needs to be focused. In an age where technology is readily accessible and available, it is important to supervise what we allow ourselves and our children to be exposed to. Without some means of 'filtering' our exposure, there is a real danger of becoming desensitised and indifferent.

Long ago, the Torah understood that self-regulation is the most powerful weapon in building a healthy society and nation and is also mankind's greatest challenge. The month of Elul is a most appropriate time to confront that challenge.

Any community dedicated to heaven will endure forever

TALMUD, Ethics of the Fathers 4:14

כל כנסיה שהיא לשם שמים סופה להתקיים

פרקי אבות ד:יד

10 January 2019
4 Shevat 5779

Dear Rabbi Marcus

On behalf of the South African Jewish community, I would like to wish you all the best on your retirement. May the incredible merit that you have accumulated through your massive contribution to Klal Yisroel be a source of overflowing blessing for you and your whole family.

You have been a visionary rabbinic leader, bringing Torah to Klal Yisroel in such an inspiring way.

You served the Waverley community in Johannesburg for many years with the greatest amount of dedication and vision, and then went on to do the same, for a remarkable 25 years, at the Central Synagogue in Great Portland Street, London.

Your active participation in promoting Holocaust remembrance is admirable, and your spearheading of educational trips to Auschwitz led to thousands of people doing the same – ensuring that this horrific tragedy is never forgotten. Your awards in this regard – including an MBE – are testament to your unwavering commitment to Holocaust education.

I so appreciate your warmth and friendship over the years, and I look forward to continuing our interactions.

I wish you continued brocha and simcha, and may Hashem bless you to continue your invaluable work in Holocaust education.

Warmest regards

Warren Goldstein

Warren Goldstein

Office of the Chief Rabbi | Union of Orthodox Synagogues of South Africa
58 Oaklands Road, Orchards 2192 Johannesburg, South Africa | P.O. Box 46559, Orange Grove 2119
T +27 10 214 2603 | F +27 11 485 1497 | E office@chiefrabbi.co.za | W www.chiefrabbi.co.za

Holocaust memorial events raise awareness

A NATION REFLECTS

Faiths hold pilgrimage

DOZENS OF Christians, Jews and Muslims marched from a mosque to an abbey via a shul as part of an interfaith initiative to rid society of prejudice, writes *Stephen Oryszczuk.*

The event, called a 'pilgrimage', was supported by senior leaders from each religion, in response to the attacks in Paris.

The brainchild of Masorti Senior Rabbi Jonathan Wittenberg, Rev. Margaret Cave and Sheikh Ibrahim Mograbi, assistant secretary-general of the Muslim Council of Britain, the walk included in

John Bercow with faith leader

There, Rabbi Marcus said event should stretch out a h while Mavis Hyman spo hushed tones about setti an eye hospital in India fo the death of her daughter in the 7/7 London bomb

Shuls organise assistance for P

Central rabbi leads 'Belarus United' mission

WEST END
JC REPORTER

JEWISH CHRONICLE 7 NOVEMBER 2014

Poles knight Auschwitz rabbi

BY SIMON ROCKER

A RABBI who has led more than 150 study missions to Auschwitz has received a Polish knighthood for his services to Holocaust education and dialogue between Jews and Poles.

Rabbi Barry Marcus was presented with the Knight's Cross of the Order of Merit by the Polish Ambassador, Witold Sobkow, in London.

Since taking his first group nearly 20 years ago, he has accompanied more than 25,000 students and teachers on visits to the Nazi death camp site. Only the day before the presentation, Rabbi Marcus had been at Auschwitz with a party of 220 students and teachers from Newcastle.

Mr Sobkow also praised his efforts towards dialogue, in particular cultural and musical events to promote Polish-Jewish reconciliation at his synagogue, the Central in London's West End. He was "a great friend of Poland. Rabbi Marcus thinks beyond borders," the ambassador said.

Rabbi Marcus — whose family came from Poland — was "humbled by this acknowledgement".

While Jews sought better understanding from others, they ought to be "a little more magnanimous" in recognising that more Poles had been declared Righteous among the Nations for saving Jews during the Holocaust than members of any other nation.

Poles had also been victims of the Nazis. "We do not have a monopoly on pain and tragedy."

The ambassador, he added, was "a genuine and true friend of us".

Rabbi Marcus (*left*) with the envoy

UK NEWS

I'm an alcoholic, I'm an addict and I'm so

BY PATRICK MAGUIRE

London Jewish News

Schools get first Holocaust primer

By JAMES KAYE

THEJC.COM

JUDAISM

A shivah is not the time for a tea party

Rabbi Barry Marcus goes through the do's and don'ts of mourning etiquette

NICOLE IN THE SADDLE FOR SYDNEY PAGE 27

AFRICAN ADVENTURE!

Husband and pregnant wife seeking asy

Synagogue aids Grozny refugees

Why it is crucial to fight the language of hate

BARRY MARCUS

To trivialise the Holocaust is to fail the millions who were murdered

Language has the power to undermine democracy

THE JEWISH CHRONICLE

Should we celebrate PM's Christian Britain?

David Cameron's view that we are a Christian nation prompted a flurry of responses. Here, two rabbis debate

Yes — BARRY MARCUS

No — JONATHAN ROMAIN

How do we find a dignified way to deal with the Shoah?

Rabbi Barry Marcus
Great Portland Street Synagogue

"Our generation is more familiar than perhaps any other with the concept of genocide"

THE TIMES WEEKEND · SATURDAY MAY

A memory of evil times

Ruth Gledhill attends a memorial service amid

JN OPINION: RABBI BARRY MARCUS, KAREN POLLOCK & SCOTT SAUNDERS

Why David's poignant plea still resonates today after 75 years

Rabbi Barry Marcus, MBE
The Central Synagogue

THE JEWISH WEEKLY — 19 APRIL 2018

"Never again" says Israeli Ambassador at Yom Hashoah commemoration

BY ADAM MOSES

Anti-Semitism is again raising its "ugly" head Israeli Ambassador Mark Regev told over 1,200 people at the annual Yom Hashoah commemoration service in Hyde Park on Sunday.

Noting where the world's longest hatred can lead, his powerful address was aimed squarely at those who espouse anti-Semitic hatred and racism.

Ambassador Regev questioned whether some people had a problem with Jews deciding to no longer be victims, defenceless, pitied or free and independent.

"Following Israel's rebirth in 1948, our people are once again able to defend ourselves, we are a free and sovereign people in our historic homeland," he exclaimed.

"Jews fleeing persecution no longer have to beg countries to open their doors. So to all those who call for Israel's destruction, whether it's the regime in Iran or its terrorist proxies, Hezbollah and Hamas, or those who express solidarity with them, including anti-Israel activists in this very country, I say this... We will protect ourselves physically from your violence and aggression, we will protect ourselves verbally from your slander and hatred, and we will continue to call out those who turned a blind eye in face of anti-Jewish bigotry.

"When the Jewish people say 'never again', we mean never again."

Henry Grunwald QC opened the hour-long ceremony with a 'defiance' theme at the National Holocaust Memorial Gardens that coincided with the 75th anniversary of the Warsaw ghetto uprising and 73rd anniversary of the liberation of Bergen-Belsen.

Chief Rabbi Ephraim Mirvis recalled examples of "heroic defiance" during The Shoah.

Calling on political leaders to send a clear message that anti-Semitism would no longer be tolerated he said there was a direct connection between leadership and defiance.

Ambassador Mark Regev

Rabbi Barry Marcus blowing the Shofar

approach to anti-Semitism. We must all remain defiant to ensure we defeat those who seek to divide us in stamping out anti-Semitism."

Board of Deputies vice president Richard Verber noted that anti-Semitism was on the rise in

Yom Hashoah UK vice-president Jacques Weisser, Holocaust survivor Gena Turgel and Game of Thrones actress Laura Pradelska gave poignant addresses.

Yom HaShoah UK ran the free event that included songs and readings.

Jews furious at church exhibition featuring Israeli checkpoint

Kaya Burgess
Religious Affairs Correspondent

A row has erupted between a Methodist church and the local Jewish community over plans to recreate a checkpoint from the Israel-Palestine border for an exhibition in the chapel.

Entitled *You cannot pass today: Life through a dividing wall*, the exhibition opens on Monday at the Hinde Street Methodist church in Marylebone, in central London. The five-day exhibition is designed to mark a world week for peace in Palestine and Israel, and will recreate the experience of queueing at a checkpoint between Jerusalem and Bethlehem, as witnessed by a preacher who visited the region this year.

The church has been forced to deny accusations from the local rabbi that the exhibition will "fan the flames of antisemitism" and has faced criticism from a Jewish rights group for causing "significant distress".

"Experience what it is like to cross a checkpoint every day. Explore how we can break down the walls that divide us so no-one lives in fear."

When the event was announced, Katherine Fox, who organised it, said London, "are shocked when I tell them what I witnessed at the checkpoint between Jerusalem and Bethlehem".

Rabbi Barry Marcus of the Central Synagogue, half a mile from the Methodist church,

"They should be ashamed" Human Rights Watch, the campaign group, has written to clergy at the church to express "dismay" at plans to "simulate security measures established by the state of Israel".

THE TIMES | Saturday September 17 2016

Miscellaneous Printed Articles and Messages

Pesach Message for B'nai B'rith Hillel Foundation
21 April 1997

Dear Friend,

Among the political passions that move the human spirit, none is capable of equalling the emotion and fervour aroused by the love of nationhood. Roughly one third of the world, over one billion people, have raised their own flags in the great dismantlement of empires since World War II, creating new nations over all the face of the earth.

We witness not grand highways leading to Utopia, but a vast complex of unstable entities that are kept in existence by the good grace of economic aid and stand constantly on the verge of erupting into turmoil. We need look no further than the former Soviet Union, Bosnia and Afghanistan. The world has become painfully aware of the fact that nationhood is not an easy art to master. With the advent of Pesach, the Festival of Freedom, it would seem to be an appropriate opportunity to pinpoint the formula for independence proposed and advocated by G-d himself.

The Haggadah records the first breakthrough in the sphere of human freedom, pointing out that man is not meant to be enslaved to his fellowman, but to be free to live, create and to exercise freedom of choice and that all are entitled to life, liberty, and the pursuit of happiness. The lesson of the exodus is quite clear. A nation is not just a people whose feeling of nationhood is based on common historical tradition or common language. Nor does the sole criteria lie in its capacity to maintain political and economic autonomy. Many majestic empires who had these qualities have disappeared leaving the world practically oblivious to the fact that they ever existed.

Our Rabbi's teach us – *Ain Lecho Ben Chorin Ela Mi Sheosek Ba'Torah* – There can be no real freedom if it is only a physical liberation, unaccompanied by spiritual aims, goals and aspirations.

The world famous scientist Professor Albert Einstein once surprised a group of Jewish parents by bestowing his personal blessing upon their children. He said, 'I would like to wish you that your children should not be men of success, but rather men of value, because men of success are going to take an awful lot out of this world, while men of value are going to put an awful lot into this world.' In those simple words, Professor Einstein crystallised the dream of nationhood, the dream of peoplehood of the Jewish people. It is that extra dimension of caring and sharing that sets a human being apart. It is that ability to relate and to be involved with the members of one's society that gives one the right to call oneself human. It is this unique combination that our tradition has called, The Living Torah.

As we celebrate the Festival of Freedom it is my hope and prayer that all members of our Community merit and experience true nationhood in the spirit of men of value who wish to uplift, to inspire and to make a better world for all of us and our children.

Wishing you all Chag Kasher V' Sameach.

Rabbi Barry Marcus

Four Questions (Pesach Booklet)
New Israel Fund
April 2001

Why is this night different from all other nights?
Seder night is one of the few occasions that can, and continues to attract and fascinate almost every Jew. Few events are as indelibly impressed on our memories as childhood and subsequent Seder nights, and few gatherings can rival the wonderful family reunions of Pesach. When thinking of Pesach the words of Heinrich Heine seem to be most appropriate – 'Jews who long have drifted from the faith of their fathers are stirred in their inmost parts when the old, familiar Passover sounds chance to fall upon their ears'. For hundreds of generations Seder night has meant the same narrative and the same ceremony and the same symbols and rituals. Yet every year there is a new generation to who it is all new and curious, and who half spontaneously and half prompted, ask the old questions and seek to elicit the answers.

Seder night is a simple illustration that it is not time that sanctifies us but it is we who have the ability to sanctify time. This is in keeping with our age old faith that seeks to translate '*Machshava*' – thought into '*Maaseh*' – deed, as Judaism is not content with leaving things only in the intellectual realm. In an effort to relive and recreate some elements of '*Yetziat mitzrayim*' – the exodus from Egypt - echoing the famous retort of Moses to Pharaoh (Exodus Chapter 10 Verse 9) 'We shall go with our young and with our old, with our sons and with our daughters' – the focus on Seder night is first and foremost the family, individually and collectively, the home and unlike other festivals, not Synagogue based. The involvement of all in preparing and participating in the Seder is the model for a 'cross generational experience' and an antidote for the so called 'generation gap'.

The beauty and attraction of Pesach, the hold Seder nights have on us, is I believe, (leaving aside the powerful impact that the concept of freedom has for us Jews) precisely because we repeat the same process from year to year. Pesach has thankfully resisted most attempts to tamper and alter it often in the name of 'modernising' by probably well-meaning but obviously misguided and ignorant individuals/organisations. This need by some to manipulate and dilute authentic Judaism is regrettable as it does not strengthen us. On the contrary it creates further divisions and weakens us.

Furthermore, the inborn failure of those who feel duty bound to unilaterally 'modernise' is poignantly expressed by a maxim I heard many years ago – 'He who marries modernity is doomed to be a widow the next day'. There is great comfort and security in knowing that certain things are immune from the ravages of time and other influences and remain steadfastly constant. This is what makes and hopefully will continue to make Seder night different and meaningful for us and future generations.

What is freedom?

Among the passions that stir the human spirit, few are capable of equalling the emotions and fervour aroused by the desire for freedom and nationhood. Roughly one third of the world, over one billion people, have raised their own flags in the great dismantlement of empires since World War Two, creating new nations all over the face of the earth.

We witness not grand highways leading to Utopia, but a vast complex of unstable entities that are kept in existence by the good grace of outside economic aid and stand constantly on the verge of erupting into turmoil. We need look no further than the former Soviet Union, the Balkans and much of Africa etc. The world has become painfully aware of the fact that freedom and nationhood is not an easy art to master.

The Haggadah records the first breakthrough in the sphere of human freedom, pointing out that man is not meant to be enslaved to or by his fellow man, but to be free to live, create and to exercise freedom of choice and that all are entitled to life, liberty, and the pursuit of happiness. The lesson of the exodus is quite clear. A nation is not just a people whose feeling of nationhood is based on common historical tradition or common language. Nor does the sole criteria lie in its capacity to maintain political and economic autonomy. Many majestic empires who had these qualities have disappeared leaving the world practically oblivious to the fact that they ever existed.

Our Rabbi's teach us – '*Ain lecho ben chorin ela mi sheosek Ba'Torah*' – There can be no real freedom if it is only a physical liberation, unaccompanied by spiritual aims, goals and aspirations.

Judaism teaches us that the lofty ideals of freedom can be achieved only through spiritual learning and living, through an ongoing commitment to Torah. Living without the spiritual dimension is often more binding, more oppressive that any form of human bondage that may be forced on us.

To the uninitiated, the Torah way of life may appear to be restrictive, but the opposite is true. These so called perceived limitations and restrictions are in fact the key to a harmonious and wholesome life, best expressed by a philosopher who once said – A violin string unattached is free yet unable to justify its existence; taut, restricted, tied in place, it suddenly gives forth melody, harmony and beauty.

For the Torah true Jew there is no 'freedom from religion' but on the contrary there is 'freedom in religion'.

How do we maintain faith in G-d during the darkest times?
Pesach is a most appropriate time to ask questions. The posing of questions in fact echoes our understanding that for us to survive we have to constantly evaluate who we are. Jewish faith is never static – always moving. All the time and simultaneously some are moving away while others often are returning like two elevators installed side by side, one moving down and out of Judaism and the other going up and back to Jewish commitment.

During periods of external threats and oppression which most would call 'dark times' we have curiously shown great resilience, creativity and unity. Many would however argue that the real 'dark times' for us are the perils of 'freedom' and affluence when our faith and adherence to it comes under severe strain and threat both from within and without. I believe we are living in such a period today when many a respected Jewish scholar would agree that in terms of faith and spirituality we are at our lowest ebb for many many years.

The number 'four' is prominent throughout the Seder – the four questions, the four cups of wine and the four sons – the wise, the sceptical, the naive and the inarticulate. Today we could sadly add a 'fifth son' – the absent one. As our faith and tradition come under severe pressure today we see more of our people drifting away from their heritage, many sadly assimilate and some even fall into the clutches of missionaries and other questionable cults. The blessings of living in a free open society are often accompanied by a weakening of Jewish commitment. To combat this and maintain our faith in G-d and strengthen our ties with our faith we need to increase our efforts to educate both young and old to lead Jewish lives with pride and dignity. This is often simply done by example as Judaism is often 'caught' and not only 'taught'.

How can I apply the lessons of the exodus to my everyday life?
One of the fascinating questions with regard to the 10 plagues is 'what was our ancestors' reaction to the pain and misery that they witnessed their Egyptian neighbours endure?' Closer scrutiny and a deeper understanding of the 9th of the 10 plagues – the plague of darkness may help guide us in an attempt to apply the lessons of the exodus to our daily lives.

Were our ancestors happy to see their oppressors suffer divine justice or were they saddened by their plight? According to the Torah, the plague of darkness was unique in that it created hardships for the Egyptians as recorded in Exodus Chapter 10 Verse 23 – 'They saw not one another, neither rose up any from his place for three days' and at the same time our forefathers were unaffected by the plague of darkness – 'And the children of Israel had light in their dwellings'. One of our Rabbinical commentators points out that the plague of darkness was unique in that it was partly self-inflicted. Instead of assisting one another during the period of darkness the Egyptians remained in their own dwellings. The inference here is that the real tragedy of the plague was the unwillingness of the Egyptians to aid each other.

Commentary points out on Chapter 11 Verse 3 – 'And the Lord gave our people favour in the sight of the Egyptians' is that our ancestors who were not stricken by darkness helped their erstwhile oppressors and supplied them with food.

The message here is clear. We as a people should never isolate ourselves from the wider community. Even if our community is safe from danger we nevertheless have an obligation to be sensitive, understanding and caring towards our neighbours in an effort to help build a just and compassionate society, and in doing so we demonstrate that we have assimilated the lessons of the exodus.

KABALA – SO WHAT'S THE BIG ATTRACTION?
South African Jewish Observer
December 2005

It is widely accepted and understood that no person can operate effectively in a vacuum.

On this subject, my late father [Harav Nochim Leib Marcus z"l formerly from Cape Town] was fond of sharing the analogy provided by the simple glass the purpose of which we all know is to hold and contain.

A human being he would say is like a glass – it too needs to be filled and this is the process we call '*chinuch*' [poorly translated to mean 'education'] – which we understand to be the ongoing process of growth and development both physical and spiritual through study, instruction, guidance and subscribing to an ethical/moral value system.

There is great danger if parents and communities neglect the education of their offspring – children will seek meaning elsewhere and this makes them susceptible, vulnerable to other influences which will not always be positive. We are all aware of the need to address our physical requirements, but sadly not all are aware of the need to nurture our spiritual component.

There is nothing invalid with searching and attempting to deepen ones knowledge per say, but one also needs to know where to go to do this, as operating out there are cults, missionary groups and others that are only too willing to ensnare, exploit and manipulate and blight the lives of many unsuspecting victims.

These cults utilize a variety of vigorous marketing and recruiting techniques – initially appealing, welcoming attractive and seductive and then often unpleasant and aggressive.

In today's 'plastic society' many cults have been quick to recognize the potency and effectiveness of recruiting a 'celebrity' to their cause as this gives them greater exposure and the ability to reach wider audiences.

Over past 50 years many such cults have surfaced offering a 'quick fix' solution to problems or alternative life styles or promises of happiness or claiming to have real answers to the perplexing questions of life. Like fads and fashion they come and go and almost always leave a trail of destruction in the aftermath. The latest such cult is the Kabbala Centres which use Kabbala and the mystery that surrounds it as a marketing ploy to attract unsuspecting victims.

Kabbala which literally means 'received' is a reference to the ancient esoteric and mystical teachings of Torah that are to be found in such texts as Sefer Hayetzirah [circa 26th century] and the Zohar [approx. 1280]. The study of Kabbala is a genuine pursuit but perforce the domain of scholars who are both mature and stable and who operate under the guidance of a recognized rabbinic authority.

Possibly because of its mystery and exclusivity people are drawn to the study of Kabbala, but as any reasonable person will understand, any kind of genuine advanced study presupposes a very solid grounding whatever the discipline. With regards Kabbala it is no different. Besides the other qualifications mentioned above, a potential student of Kabbala needs amongst others to have a deep and substantial understanding of Chumash and Nach and other holy texts. He or she also needs to be fluent in Hebrew and Aramaic which in reality can only be obtained after years of study at a recognized and genuine place of learning. In effect the study of Kabbala is a closed door and mostly inaccessible to the average layman.

Cults like the Kabbala Centre and similar organizations will, despite this, have the ignorant and naive believe the opposite. They will insist there is no problem here – after all we live in the age of the 'quick fix', where instant remedies are available for all situations. They maintain that they can make the study of Kabbala accessible to all and sundry-ignorant Jew and non-Jew alike.

The lure of unlocking the secrets of the Kabbala along with rubbing shoulders with celebrities can sadly prove overwhelming for the many well-meaning but vulnerable in today's world.

Organisations peddling so called Kabbala, target and exploit the ignorance of many an alienated Jew or non-Jew duping people into believing there are shortcuts including the ridiculous claim that in order to plumb the depths of Kabbala, one does not need prior knowledge of Hebrew, and that it is simply sufficient to scan the ancient Hebrew and Aramaic texts.

These ridiculous claims are tantamount to being told at school that you do not require a basic understanding of arithmetic and science in order to master quantum physics.

Whereas these stupid claims are precisely that, and may be seen as harmless, there is a darker side to their activities. When cults and organisations consistently exploit people's ignorance and vulnerability, enriching only themselves in the process, while so many of their followers are relieved of vast sums of money, or become 'foot soldiers' peddling all kinds of dubious wares such as worthless pieces of ribbon bracelets and books at exorbitant prices, or encouraged to stop taking medication and rather drink 'holy water', then we are obviously no longer faced with just another quaint harmless operation or organization but a dangerous cult as the Kabbala centre has in fact been listed in the USA.

For the unsuspecting, the problem is further exacerbated by so called and self-styled charismatic 'authority' figures who coupled with celebrity interest makes for a dangerous cocktail.

Whilst the quest for meaning and knowledge and the search for truth is admirable and to be encouraged, one needs to be extremely careful to whom one entrusts oneself as there are sadly many a charlatan and cults who are not accountable to anyone or recognized authority waiting to deceive the unsuspecting amongst us.

So if one is curious and hungry for genuine Jewish knowledge where should one go? Save yourself heartache and go directly to the source – as is stated in Pirkei Avot [The Ethics of the Fathers] Chapter 6 Mishnah 25 – '*hafoch ba d'chula ba*' – 'Study Torah again and again for everything is in it' and to get there ask your local Rabbi who I am sure will only be glad to guide you and point you in the right direction.

Auschwitz Theft: Sign of Times

Jewish Chronicle
25 December 2009

The joy of our Chanukah celebrations was dampened when we awoke on the 7th day of Chanukah to learn of the distressing theft of the infamous sign 'Arbeit Macht Frei' from the gates at the entrance of Auschwitz I.

Coincidentally, our Torah reading on the 7th day of Chanukah mentions the tribe of Ephraim. In Jeremiah Chapter 31, Ephraim is referred to as *Haben Yakir Li Ephraim* – 'Ephraim is my most precious son, a delightful child that whenever I speak of him I remember him more and more'. The thoughts of many survivors and others were sadly deflected away from the light of Chanukah to the dark days of the Shoah and found themselves forcibly reflecting on precious family members lost at the hands of the Nazis and their accomplices.

The expression '*Arbeit macht frei*' which literally means 'Work Makes Free' or 'Work Liberates' was first used in 1872 by Lorenz Diefenbach, the German Nationalist author, but later embraced by the Nazi Party when it came to power in 1933.

The same slogan was placed at the entrance of a number of Nazi camps including Dachau, Sachsenhausen and Theresienstadt. However, it is the 16ft sign over the entrance to Auschwitz I which has come to symbolise the horrors of the Holocaust and has become one of the most tangible and visible reminders of the Nazi tyranny.

This instantly recognisable sign, has stood in its place since 1940 when the camp's first Commander, Rudolf Höss, placed it there. Whether the motive in stealing this sign was part of some lurid fascination with Holocaust memorabilia or for financial gain or for a more sinister reason, the speed at which the Polish authorities have recovered the sign is to be acknowledged. We hope the culprits will be punished accordingly.

The stolen sign, which has now been recovered, adorned the entrance to Auschwitz I which was originally an army barracks but was later enlarged by the Nazis to hold Jews, Polish political prisoners, war prisoners, Gypsies and others. It was, 3 km away from Auschwitz I, in the purpose built killing factory Auschwitz II, also known as Birkenau, where over a million Jews and others were gassed and incinerated.

Though most people will be visually familiar with this sign even before visiting Auschwitz, either from books, films or documentaries, our Rabbi's point out in the Midrash, *Eino domeh re'iyah l'shemiyah* – hearing about something is not like seeing it. However well a visitor to Auschwitz may think he is prepared, the truth is, nothing can prepare one adequately.

I have watched on countless occasions how both students and adults upon entering Auschwitz I are stopped in their tracks when entering the camp as if completely transfixed by this duplicitous sign that has become synonymous with the unspeakable acts of evil that occurred just beyond the sign. Once you move under the sign, along the double barbed wire fences, you are no longer reading from a book or watching a documentary but you become enveloped and surrounded by evil of an unimaginable scale. I have witnessed initial discomfort on people's faces turn into anguish, numbness and an overwhelming sense of disbelief.

I hope the sign is speedily restored, not only for the obvious reasons but also to retain crucial and vital evidence in the face of the grotesque phenomenon known as Holocaust denial.

Only last week in Copenhagen, world leaders attempted to tackle controversial environmental issues. The theft of this sign may be a further indication that what we equally need is to effect a 'climate change' in Europe and further afield due to increased levels of anti-Semitism. What is abundantly clear is that the theft of the sign confirms the need for continued education both here in the United Kingdom and worldwide.

Reality Prevents the Shoah from Becoming Yesterday's News

The Jewish News
8 April 2010

This Sunday the Jewish world will be called on to mark Yom HaShoah. In our calendar this day is 27 Nisan, the anniversary of the Warsaw Ghetto uprising and the day that has been set aside to remember victims of the Holocaust.

Whereas Holocaust Memorial Day, which was recently established by the government in the United Kingdom (and elsewhere) is linked to the liberation of Auschwitz-Birkenau on 27 January 1945 and aimed at a wider audience, Yom HaShoah has, for a number of decades, been the designated day of private grief and remembrance for Jewish communities worldwide and is deeply embedded in our collective consciousness.

Today, 65 years after the end of the Second World War, I would have thought it not unreasonable to have expected Yom HaShoah, in whatever format or on whatever date, to be marked on similar lines to, say, Remembrance Sunday.

This annual event in November features dignified ceremonies recalling a dark period in human history and is not blighted by denials, disrespect and boycotts from some sections of the population.

I often ask if it is extravagant, preposterous or simply absurd, in an age of such great technological advances, to expect a similar parallel leap and advancement in maybe not entirely eradicating anti-Semitism and other forms of prejudice, but at the very least curbing or minimising it?

Sadly, there has been a resurgence of anti-Semitism, as confirmed by the latest figures published recently by the CST – reflecting similar trends in Europe and elsewhere.

Some two weeks ago I noticed that the BBC, in its wisdom, saw fit to include in one of its recent Sunday programmes a discussion on whether it is now time to draw a line under the Holocaust. Would the BBC, I wonder, countenance a similar discussion on the subject of Remembrance Sunday?

Only those with ostrich-like tendencies can, at their peril, ignore the subtle and shameless increase in hostility towards Jews worldwide – often under the guise of anti-Israel sentiment.

Recent noises from the Obama administration in Washington, even suggested a possible link between Israel and the deaths of US soldiers in Afghanistan, is all too familiar.

Reverting to language and propaganda that unashamedly paints Jews as scapegoats for the ills of the world, merely serves to further embolden those with an already hostile agenda and an antagonistic and often biased and irresponsible media.

How profoundly disappointing it is when the president of the United States is more concerned with Jews building homes in Jerusalem than Iran building nuclear weapons.

Iran's leader is regularly given platforms to deny the Holocaust and in the same breath threaten another Shoah.

We face an unholy alliance of so-called leftwing liberals, radical Islam, the BNP and an antagonistic media exploiting age-old prejudices, often bolstered by what, of late, seems to be compulsory appearances by some self-hating Jews including washed-up Jewish MPs and others of the same ilk.

Do we hear the same motley group voicing opposition to events in Darfur, Sudan or Zimbabwe or encouraging boycotts against goods from China, Iran or Saudi Arabia, or musicians from Sudan or Zimbabwe?

However much we may wish to, or are encouraged to do so, our reality prevents us from viewing the Shoah as a historical aberration never to be repeated again.

On Yom Hashoah we need to pay homage to the victims of the Shoah and pay tribute to the ever-decreasing survivors, but also reflect on our need to display courage and resolve in standing up against anti-Semitism, hatred and prejudice in all its forms – for our sake and for the sake of all humanity.

Why is it Crucial to Fight the Language of Hate

The Jewish Chronicle
25 June 2010

I cannot imagine any JC reader for whom the words 'Holocaust' and 'Nazi' do not resonate. These are words with terrible connotations that speak of the darkest night we have ever endured. We do not use them lightly. When we hear them used in inappropriate or even trivial contexts, we feel wounded.

In recent years, we have relatedly been confronted by the poison of Holocaust denial. Courageous people like Deborah Lipstadt have proven in court that Holocaust denial cannot hide behind the right to freedom of expression. British law recognises that language – the language of hate – has the power to undermine the foundations of democratic societies. The language of Holocaust denial is an insidious form of antisemitism with implications not just for Jews, but for anyone concerned with human rights and democratic values.

But it is not only the deniers who threaten the memory of the Holocaust. By calling an anti-smoking local councillor 'a Nazi', the broadcaster Jon Gaunt could be taken as implying that National Socialism is an ideology characterised by mere officiousness, and deemphasising the hatred and murder at its heart. And, as recent elections here have sadly shown, along with the resurgence of far-right extremism across Europe, there are still people who subscribe to that noxious brand of politics. We need to remain vigilant.

The scale of the Holocaust and its impact on Jewish communities across Europe remain unimaginable. When apparently respectable politicians compare events in the Middle East to the Holocaust, it is insulting. Such trivialisation of the Holocaust desecrates the memory of the millions of victims of Nazi tyranny, and offends the memories of those who survived.

If we fail to understand the lasting relevance of the Shoah to our lives, then we fail the millions who were murdered. That is why the Holocaust Educational Trust's Lessons from Auschwitz project is so important.

When, in 1996, I began arranging visits to Auschwitz-Birkenau for the Jewish community, I did so in the initial belief that it was important for Jews to understand their own history. But this particular history is significant not only for Jews. In 1999, the Holocaust Educational Trust began to take students and teachers of all backgrounds to Auschwitz, affirming that the

Holocaust is part of the story of humanity. It has been a privilege to have been able to take part in these visits and to have led ceremonies at the Birkenau crematoria.

Visiting the site where more than a million people were murdered can be a transformative experience. I can testify to the positive impact that it has had on thousands of students and teachers. When, at the crematoria, I ask the students to consider not 'where was G-d at Auschwitz?' but 'where was man?', their reactions never cease to move me.

Now, with government support, the trust takes sixth-form students from every school in the country. Organising up to 17 visits annually, the HET has just achieved a remarkable milestone: the 10,000th student has now participated in Lessons from Auschwitz. All the young participants gain not only a deeper knowledge of the Holocaust itself, but also an understanding of why it is so important to oppose prejudice today.

A Shivah is Not the Time For a Tea Party
The Jewish Chronicle
23 July 2010

Rabbi Barry Marcus goes through the do's and don'ts of mourning etiquette.

A colleague once told me about a call he received from a congregant informing him of the death of a family member. Before the rabbi could even offer his condolences, he was asked if he could recommend a good caterer for the one-night shivah.

All communal rabbis face a daily challenge in dealing with the lifecycle events in their communities, whether births, bar/bat mitzvahs, weddings or sadly, bereavements. All these events are charged with various levels of emotion which demand sensitive handling.

Despite different levels of knowledge, understanding or observance, I believe most people are keen to do that which is right and correct when it comes to dealing with the death of a loved one.

Halachah (Jewish law) talks about the *ikar* – the fundamental essence of the law or custom, and the *tafel* – the secondary or less important.

Communities often cultivate their own customs: some are not in keeping with our traditional beliefs and practices and some in our Anglo Jewish community often latch on to the less important practices at the expense of more important ones.

The most important issue in bereavement is the dignity of the deceased and that entails doing absolutely everything to bring a person to burial as soon as possible. All too often this fundamental principle is overlooked: it has been my colleagues' experience that many a funeral is unjustifiably postponed for the wrong reasons.

It is considered an indignity initially to leave a body unattended and likewise to allow it to languish in a mortuary for a number of days, for example in order to enable a distant relative or friend to be present at the funeral. This is why in Jerusalem for instance, funerals take place even at night.

It is equally important to give respect to the deceased by sitting shivah – which means 'seven', for a week – and saying Kaddish for the eleven-month period. Here too, all too often, a variety of inappropriate practices are to be found, some of which were highlighted in Steven Berkoff's recent comic play, 'Sit and Shiver'.

The purpose of having a minyan at a mourner's home, is first and foremost because the mourner is meant to stay indoors for the first seven days of the mourning period. In order to help mourners fulfil this obligation, a minyan is then made at their house, which thereby saves them going to shul.

But in many parts of our community, the popular perception is that shivah means anything but seven, and usually means 'eight' i.e. that we have prayers at eight o'clock and only at eight o'clock, as if this 'prayer frequency' is only available at that time throughout the year.

One needs to make a distinction between making a minyan for the mourner and the obligation to comfort a mourner. One can offer comfort to a mourner at any time of the day during the shivah period and beyond. In fact, holding prayers at eight o'clock in winter is counterproductive as only the ma'ariv service can be recited, which means that any mourner who desires to fulfil his obligation in terms of shivah and Kaddish, has to leave his home and go to shul to pray minchah and say Kaddish. The correct practice is to have a minyan in the mourner's home, morning, afternoon and evening throughout the week of shivah.

The slavish devotion to eight o'clock prayers, which invariably turns into a tea party, is again not in keeping with Jewish practice. The inevitable socialising that accompanies the prayers is totally inappropriate and insensitive to mourners, as the purpose of one's presence at the house of mourning is to console the mourner and not an opportunity to indulge in small talk and petty gossip. According to Jewish practice, if we go to a house of mourning, we are meant simply to sit down in their presence and wait for them (if they so desire) to speak to us first. If we were all to follow this practice, many an uncomfortable and embarrassing situation would be avoided.

Comments I have heard directed at a mourner such as 'Oh well, don't worry – they're better off where they are now' are certainly out of place. Initially remaining silent is part of Judaism's sensitivity to the mourner, as in most cases a mourner does not desire to indulge in any, and certainly not idle, talk. This is also one of the reasons a mourner, on returning from the cemetery, eats an egg which has no 'mouth', reflecting their traumatic state. We are meant only on leaving to console the mourner with the traditional words, 'May the Almighty comfort and console you amongst the rest of the mourners of Zion and Jerusalem'.

The pressure that mourners often feel to provide food is also out of step with correct Jewish practice. All the mourner's needs should be taken care of, not only in offering them tea and coffee, but by the provision of all meals during the seven day period, and not the other way round.

The practice of sitting shivah for seven days is designed to help the mourners through a difficult period. I find it curious that many a psychologist has marvelled and expressed admiration for our age-old practices, for they have recognised how effective the process is in dealing with bereavement, yet we often turn our backs and lose an opportunity to find genuine comfort and consolation.

As someone who ran a crisis centre for many years, I can testify to many a mourner who was plagued and scarred as a consequence of not going through the process of mourning.

In dealing with death and bereavement, we would all do well to be mindful of the statement in the Gemara, (tractate *Berachot*) that 'kindness is the highest form of wisdom'.

How Do We Find a Dignified Way to Deal With the Shoah?

Jewish News
22 March 2012

With the words of Megillat Esther still echoing in our ears, particularly the genocidal intention of Haman in his stated declaration 'To exterminate all Jews, young and old, children and women' (Chapter 3 Verse 13), we cannot escape the fact that sadly, it is our generation, possibly more than any other, that is more familiar and better placed to understand the concept of genocide.

The question is of course, 'Do we want to confront and to comprehend, are we motivated to find an appropriate and dignified way of dealing with the Shoah?' These are the very questions which, I believe, are on the mind of our fast dwindling group of Survivors.

There is, at present, a distinct unease in the Jewish world, especially in Israel, with the all too familiar rhetoric and threats of genocide emanating from Iran, the Persia of Old.

Our disquiet is exacerbated by the fact that we are not dealing with some marginal or insignificant individual, but the President of a sovereign state who has on numerous occasions shamefully been offered international platforms, at the UN and elsewhere and has consistently denied the Shoah, yet in the same breath threatens another Holocaust on Jews in Israel and worldwide.

We are understandably somewhat anxious as recent history has clearly exposed the limitations and danger of inactivity and appeasement.

As a people, we are not defined by the Shoah, but in our community we need to nevertheless find an appropriate response and a dignified locus in our consciousness for the Shoah.

I cannot help but highlight the anomaly that since pioneering the concept of one day educational visits to Auschwitz-Birkenau in 1997, when it was initially my wish to take every single Jew and Jewess in the UK (and many hundreds have responded positively), the reality is that I have now taken more non-Jews than Jews thanks to the Holocaust Educational Trust and Government support. Yet whilst literally tens of thousands have participated in these day visits, we cannot help but notice that over the past few years the various Yom HaShoah ceremonies appear to attract fewer and fewer participants.

Despite the availability and accessibility that modern air travel offers us, still relatively small numbers of people are prepared to visit a death or concentration camp. As our Rabbis point out succinctly, 'hearing is not like seeing' (Midrash Shemot 19) – we need to see for ourselves however uncomfortable and painful, if only to strengthen our resolve not to forget the memory of the millions of our brothers and sisters who were so mercilessly butchered. I believe that we cannot face the challenges of the future without adequately confronting our past.

I nevertheless understand that it may be unrealistic for each and every one of us in our community to visit Holocaust sights whether Auschwitz or elsewhere but equally frustrating is the apathy and apparent disconnect that so many seem to have adopted ignoring the fact that only 21 miles of water separated the United Kingdom from the horrors of the Shoah on mainland Europe.

Is it too much to ask for 2 hours a year to pay tribute to, to remember and to honour our ever dwindling but heroic Survivors?

Simply put, if someone passes on, most decent people I am sure, would take the trouble to attend either the funeral, the shiva or find an hour to pay one's respects. Surely it is not unreasonable to do so on Yom HaShoah (as distinct from Holocaust Memorial Day on 27th January which is a government led initiative aimed mainly at, and for the benefit of, the wider society). If we will not do so, who will then pay respect for the millions of nameless and innocent victims of the Nazis and their collaborators? If not us, who will support our Survivors? Who will be the guardians of our collective memory?

If we seek understanding from the wider world and expect sensitivity for our genocide, I believe, we need to embrace Yom HaShoah somewhat more vigorously.

This year we have an opportunity to do precisely this by either attending the special ceremony at JFS on Wednesday 18th April or at the Dell in Hyde Park on Sunday 22nd April at 11:00 am.

Why David's Poignant Plea Still Resonates Today After 75 Years
The Jewish News
22 January 2015

Some years ago, Yad Vashem initiated a campaign called 'Guardian of the Memory' in an attempt to ensure victims of the Shoah should never be forgotten.

The wider community was encouraged to 'adopt' a Holocaust victim and light a candle on Holocaust Memorial Day in his or her memory.

A modest and simple publication was distributed as part of the campaign, which included a brief yet poignant excerpt from the last letter of David Berger written before his murder by the Nazis in Vilna in 1941: 'I should like someone to remember that there once lived a person named David Berger.'

David's desperate and simple plea, written under the most perilous of conditions, resonates with us because it so succinctly expresses one of our greatest conscious and subconscious fears and anxieties – that of being forgotten.

As the 70-year anniversary of the end of the Shoah draws closer, it is a most appropriate opportunity to focus on how to deal with this dark chapter in our history and that of humanity.

Questions and issues, such as what place the Shoah should hold in our lives and in the future, and how we deal with issues of memory and remembrance, are but a few of those that need to be addressed.

The reality is, of course, that survivors and many in the field of Holocaust education are constantly preoccupied with these very challenges.

When one speaks and interacts with survivors – with all their many tortuous memories and traumas – one almost always senses that the fear of being forgotten is ever present, even if unspoken.

As a people, we are not defined by the Shoah, but we need to find a most befitting and effective way of responding to and locating a dignified locus in our consciousness for it.

The many remarkable and dedicated individuals and organisations involved in the Shoah, and specifically with keeping its memory alive, are all dreading the time when there are no survivors and living witnesses around.

We have all been inspired by their personal dignity and humbled by their absence of bitterness and a desire for revenge.

When we have had sadly to contend with the perversion called Holocaust denial, attempts to obfuscate, trivialise and dilute the Shoah, when politicians, the media and others who should know better use insulting and insensitive Nazi terms and insignia, we are fortified by the presence and voices of these extraordinary survivors at our side.

Our concern at a future without survivors is matched only by our consternation at the rise of anti-Semitic incidents both in the UK and in Europe, especially in France of late. Anti-Semitism mutates and appears in different guises.

In the Middle Ages, we were persecuted for our faith; then, in the 20th century, for our race.

Today, that same hatred is aimed at the Jewish state, at Israel, the only country among the 193 that make up the United Nations whose right to exist is routinely challenged and in many quarters denied.

Many of the recent anti-Semitic incidents and the targets of terror in Europe have all too often not been Israeli government offices, but synagogues, Jewish schools, cemeteries and museums – places not of Israeli policy-making, but of ordinary local Jewish life.

We all hoped some of the recent scenes of the kind witnessed in France and elsewhere had been consigned to history; the fact that they weren't behoves us all to redouble our efforts to make sure our world will not be blighted again by the horrors of the Shoah.

We need to try to reach as many people as possible and educate as many as possible to the dangers that come with silence and inactivity and to encourage as many as possible to hear the pleas of the voiceless innocent millions, such as David Berger.

I have accompanied almost all the Holocaust Educational Trust's visits to Poland as part of its Lessons from Auschwitz project, which have allowed thousands of young people to bear witness to man's inhumanity, but our work is not done.

On this 70th anniversary of the Shoah, it is essential to pay homage to its victims and salute the decreasing number of survivors.

But also to reflect on our need to display courage and resolve in standing up against anti-Semitism, hatred and prejudice in all their forms – for our sake and that of all humanity.

RABBI BARRY

MATCHMAKING – Rabbi Barry is God's gift to singletons and errant fashion designers.

Interview by PENNY MARTIN
Portraits by BRUNO STAUB

RABBI BARRY MARCUS
Rabbi at London's Central Synagogue
Born in Cape Town, South Africa
Lives in London, England

RABBI BARRY MARCUS is the progressive force of London's Central Synagogue. Indeed, he was the risk-taking humanist who guided designer JOHN GALLIANO back to good spiritual health after his tipsy rant in a Parisian bar. BARRY grew up in South Africa, where his ground-breaking crisis centre created ructions over its multi-ethnic stance in the 1980s. An inveterate matchmaker, RABBI BARRY can introduce you to any eligible Jewish singleton in a tweet.

PENNY: Our chat at the MAISON MARGIELA show in London, where we were sat next to each other in January, was one of the most unexpected conversations I've had on the front row. Another editor came up to me and asked what we had been talking about.

BARRY: I'd never been to a fashion show previously. I can't say it was at the top of my list. But in life you must be open to everything, within reason. I deliberated when JOHN GALLIANO invited me. But with this being his first show, his re-entry into his passion, I thought, if he wants me there, then who am I not to help maybe one of the greatest design talents to flourish again?

P: How did you meet him?

B: After his unfortunate outburst in a restaurant some years ago, he'd reached out to the Jewish community in Paris, but they took the moral high ground and shunned him. So after an approach was made to the Anti-Defamation League in New York, its director, ABE FOXMAN, introduced me to the proprietor of Condé Nast, JONATHAN NEWHOUSE, who brought JOHN here. I designed a sort of course, part of which involved spending time with a Holocaust survivor. JOHN also asked if he could come to a service in the synagogue; he'd never been. I mean, his knowledge of Jews and Judaism was actually very limited...

P: I have to confess: so is mine. I'd no idea the synagogue was even here right in the centre of London.

B: The first time JOHN came to synagogue on Shabat, we had to warn him that he shouldn't dress so flamboyantly. I mean, he has the most wonderful sense of dress. He's come in some of the most amazing outfits – the berets, the fancy scarves. The first time my secretary let him in, she didn't know who he was. Her eyes were out on stalks!

P: How did it go?

B: Well, my work with him had been done in private – it was my decision and no one's business. But I've got Holocaust survivors in the synagogue, so taking JOHN there was a risk. And you shouldn't think I didn't get flak. One or two people recognised him and said to me, 'What's he doing in here?' I know cynics say his motivation for seeing me was to restore his reputation. But over time, we built up a relationship and I'm absolutely satisfied that to brand him as an anti-Semite would be an injustice. As a human being, as a Jew, as a rabbi, as a humanist, I'm almost duty-bound to open the door to somebody that wants to make amends.

P: So what did you think of the MARGIELA show?

B: I've seen clips of fashion shows on TV and some of our community are involved in the industry, so I wasn't walking into a blind alley. I can't say I understand the intricacies that go into making a garment, but the show was very impressive, a smooth operation; perhaps more modest and dignified than what I'd seen before. It almost belied the notion you have of fashion: people getting excited about things that aren't really important in life.

P: You say you're not fully aware of fashion's intricacies, but when we met, you said that clothing was in your blood.

B: Yes, my grandfather was a tailor. It saved him in a sense – he sensed what was coming in the 1930s and his profession helped him get out of Slonim in Poland and into Africa. I grew up in South Africa, and many of my uncles were in the clothing trade. One still has a factory making ladies fashions in Cape Town; all of our school uniforms were bought from another uncle. But my grandfather made my first few suits. I looked after them for years and years because they were the product of his hands, his labour.

P: What's that Yiddish word, is it *schmatters?*

B: It's a very warm, colloquial term for the clothing industry. A *schmatta* is a rag, an off-cut, so *schmatters* means rag trade. Though it refers to something quite lowly, it's said with some reverence, as *schmatters* was one of the trades that Jews could engage in when we were prohibited from participating in other things. In fact, this area of London was its *schmatta* centre; 20 years ago I could walk down Great Portland Street and meet half of my community. So clothes are important to me. In fact tomorrow I'm going down to MOSS BROS. to get my morning suit fitted for next week, when I'm getting my MBE at the Palace.

(Phone notification sounds)

P: Please answer it. We can pause the recording.

B: No, no. I need to put this on silent. It's probably just my WhatsApp.

P: You're a WhatsApp user?

B: Yeah, I love it. It allows me to be in touch with people all over the world and you can respond when you want to. It's not like a telephone.

P: I saw on your synagogue's website that you use digital media quite extensively, with little films to explain different principles of the faith. Is there much demand for that?

B: Oh yeah, the emails are incessant... On Friday we had a Muslim guy who'd become a Christian and wanted to learn a bit more about Judaism, and today there's a query about what place dreams have in Jewish life. And did you see that school party as you were arriving? Some synagogues prefer not to have people coming and going, but so long as it's not a security risk, we encourage it. I put together a little book for people who are not Jewish so they don't feel like idiots in there.

P: It's quite a service you're providing. Why do you feel it's so important to respond to non-Jewish people's approaches? It's my understanding that the Reform movement in Judaism has a policy of not encouraging conversion.

B: We are absolutely not in favour of proselytising. For us, there's no greater act of arrogance. Knocking on people's doors reduces faith to the work of a second-hand vacuum-cleaner salesman. Our approach is: whatever you are, just be a good one.

P: Then why lay yourself open to flak, as you put it, for introducing different people of different faiths, or JOHN GALLIANO, into the synagogue?

B: Let me put it this way: when I was knighted by the Polish government last year for my work in their country...

P: I read you started a programme of taking non-Jewish people to Auschwitz at the end of the '90s. How many times have you been?

B: 150 trips now; 25,000 people. I'm going again tomorrow with 250 students and teachers from Cardiff. Anyway, in his speech, the Polish ambassador, WITOLD SOBKÓW, said my award was for thinking beyond borders. I was the first Orthodox rabbi to invite a German ambassador into synagogue on a Sabbath morning, for instance. I wasn't trying to be sensationalist – it's more that I honestly believe that whatever we've tried so far hasn't worked.

P: Worked in what sense?

B: There's still such a disconnect. You go onto the internet and there's so much anti-Semitism and bitterness. So we have to do something to break down these preconceptions. I got flak for the German ambassador, of course, but I'm absolutely resolute that I'm doing the right thing.

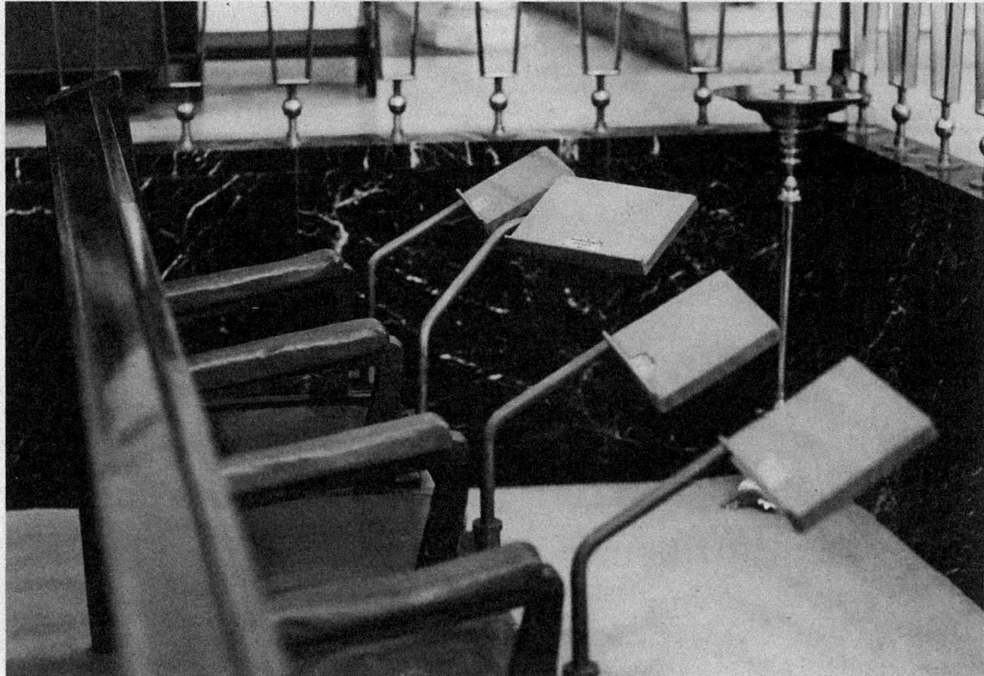

— The interior of the Central Synagogue contains a sort of VIP front row, pictured, for the most prestigious attendees.

RABBI BARRY

— The pictured sheer curtain, known as a MECHITZA, is used to divide men and women of the congregation during the synagogue's three daily services.

P: It must be a heavy burden — I read you visit Auschwitz every week at this time of year.

B: I try not to let it overwhelm me, or to be seen as representing only that. So I also go to the theatre, I watch sport and often, after services, I'll zip away on my bicycle and go to the gym.

P: What do you do there?

B: I'll be on the treadmill or on the cross-trainer. After 45 minutes of that, I'll come back, have a shower and go into meetings. There are things you can't legislate for, of course — the funerals, the crises in people's lives. But then there are nice things, like seeing couples that are about to be married.

P: I gather you're a bit of a matchmaker.

B: Where did you pick that up?

P: Not a particularly reputable source, admittedly. A Bangladeshi dating site, I think.

B: Well, it's not complete nonsense. Introductions are part of my pastoral duties, of course. Only today I put a young guy together with a girl in America. He's 26, a law graduate, and is going to fly over there to meet her. The mother sent me a text saying her daughter...here, I'll show it to you...and in this case, someone in my community had recommended this guy. It's just a case of her family wanting to know what he's like: do I know his family, has he got good qualities, is he stable?

P: You must appreciate that to most people, the idea of your mother getting involved in your romantic life is a complete nightmare. Let alone your rabbi.

B: Look, all I'm doing is responding to a request. I'd never preach that if you're single, you're not welcome. But if someone wants to find a partner, then there's nothing wrong in it.

P: Are you aware of Jewish dating sites and apps like JDate, JSwipe and Yenta?

B: Yes, I've married couples that met on JDate. It's obviously the difference between an animate and an inanimate interaction and a lot of people using them don't tell the truth and there are weirdos. But overall, I think there are more positives than negatives. When I was growing up, meeting people wasn't a problem — you went to a beach, you went to a party and you met people! Now it's not so easy; people are stuck to their phones or PCs, and many of their relationships aren't real. But in a sense, the web is only doing what rabbis have done for centuries.

P: What makes you particularly good at engineering those introductions?

B: I'm actually in a strange position, since I'm one of the very few rabbis who are divorced. Normally, a community wouldn't even consider you, as they want the full package. I've got five daughters, but people also want the wife. I was lucky that the previous chief rabbi, LORD JONATHAN SACKS, looked beyond all that. Even so, the first wedding I did after my divorce was extremely emotional for me, because I was officiating in circumstances where I am actually a bit of a failure. But it does give me some understanding of how tricky relationships can be.

P: Does it also mean that you are now the one who gets introduced? Do people try to set up the Divorced Rabbi?

B: Yes, they do. When I first arrived here, I received many lovely invitations to functions but very often I'd be plunked next to some eligible... They'd wheel out the cousin who was on the shelf. Sometimes it was painful as neither she nor I would be forewarned and we'd be stuck together for a two-hour dinner, where it was obvious that neither of us was right for the other. When introductions are made in such a contrived way, it can be mortifying. So the secret, I quickly learnt, is to be sure to ask who will be sitting at your table, before you accept.